Business Management
for Engineers

Business Management for Engineers

*How I Overcame My Moment of Inertia
and Embraced the Dark Side*

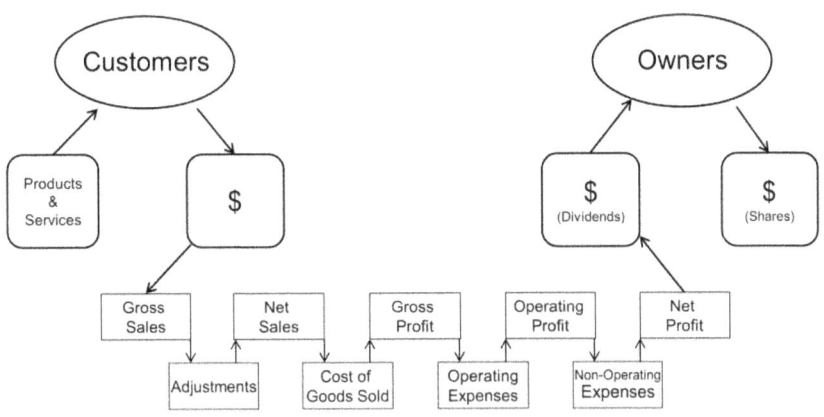

Alan C. Tribble, PhD

with Alan F. Breitbart, MBA

Copyright 2018 by Alan C. Tribble.

Cover design by Ellen Holt.

All rights reserved. No part of this book shall be reproduced, stored in a retrieval system, or transmitted by any means; electronic, mechanical, photocopying, recording or otherwise, without written permission from the publisher, except for providing a direct quote and providing reference to this book.

Quantity discounts and custom editions are available.

Email: alantribble@gmail.com

or visit:

    www.businessmanagementforengineers.com

where you can also download additional resources.

ISBN 978-1-7321545-0-6

Resources available at

BusinessManagementForEngineers.com

include

- Highlights from the book

- Copies of the tables and slides for academic users

- Copies of annual reports referenced in the book

- Webinar summary of each chapter

Table of Contents

List of Figures v

List of Tables vii

   Acknowledgments ix

   Preface xi

   CHAPTER 1 – INTRODUCTION 1
      The Four Factors of Production 1
      Free and Controlled Markets 5

   CHAPTER 2 – THE BUSINESS OF BUSINESS 9
      Stock Markets 10
      Financial Accounting 17
         Discretionary Spending 25
      Cost Accounting 28
      Pricing 36
      Value Proposition 41
      Business Model 44
      Forecasting 46

   CHAPTER 3 – NAVIGATING THE CORPORATION 53
      Organizational Structure 57
      Organizational Hierarchy 68

   CHAPTER 4 – RULES OF THE ROAD 73
      Example: US Laws and Regulations 75
         Taxation 78
         Intellectual Property 79
         Federal Acquisition Regulation System 82
      Budgeting & Planning 92
      Government Purchasing Methodology 100
      Fiscal and Monetary Policy 104

CHAPTER 5 – GLOBALIZATION: WORKING INTERNATIONALLY 107
- US Export Regulations 110
  - International Traffic in Arms Regulations (ITAR) 110
  - Export Administration Regulations (EAR) 118
- Foreign Import Regulations 120
- Currency Exchange Rates 123
- Cultural Differences 126

CHAPTER 6 – PLANNING FOR SUCCESS 131
- Concept Definition 131
  - The Technical Aspect 132
  - The Business Case 136
  - The Budget Aspect 145
- Program Management 146
  - Scope 152
  - Time 160
  - Cost 162
  - Quality 163
  - Human Resources 164
  - Risk (and Opportunity) 165
  - Communications 168
  - Procurement 170
  - Stakeholders 170
  - Integration 171
- Business Development 172
  - Sales 172
  - Marketing 175
  - Strategy 177

CHAPTER 7 – EVALUATING SUCCESS 179
- Project Success – Earned Value Management 179
- Making EVM Work 186
- Portfolio Success – BCG Matrix 193
- Business Unit Success – GE / McKinsey Matrix 197
- Corporate Success – Stock Price 199

Appendix – Laws and Regulations Affecting Aviation and Space Exploration 205

Index 211

Acronyms 213

Other Publications by Alan Tribble 217

List of Figures

Figure 1.	Sales, Profit, and Other Measures of Financial Performance.	19
Figure 2.	Balancing the Needs of Customers and Owners.	25
Figure 3.	Examples of Discretionary Expenses.	26
Figure 4.	Boeing Executive Committee.	54
Figure 5.	Airbus Group Executive Committee.	54
Figure 6.	NASA Organizational Structure.	55
Figure 7.	FAA Organizational Structure.	55
Figure 8.	Example Functional Areas.	57
Figure 9.	Example Hierarchy	68
Figure 10.	Vertical and Horizontal Organizational Structures.	71
Figure 11.	The US Government Budget Approval Process.	94
Figure 12.	The US DoD Budget Cycle.	97
Figure 13.	Example Program Element Listing from the US DoD Budget.	98
Figure 14.	The DoD Project Life Cycle.	99
Figure 15.	The Process of Completing a Foreign Military Sale.	117
Figure 16.	Currency Exchange Rate, US Dollars to EUROs.	124
Figure 17.	Notional Business Case – Investment and Return on Investment.	138
Figure 18.	Specific business case	141
Figure 19.	Example Cash Flow.	144

Figure	Title	Page
Figure 20.	Systems and Software Engineering, System Life Cycle Processes.	147
Figure 21.	Systems Engineering and Project Control.	147
Figure 22.	A Notional Schedule.	161
Figure 23.	Reliability Relation for Series and Parallel Components.	163
Figure 24.	The Sales Funnel.	173
Figure 25.	A Simple Marketing Example.	177
Figure 26.	Cost vs Time for a Project with a Linear Work Rate.	181
Figure 27.	Actual Cost Growing at a Rate Below That of the Work Scheduled.	182
Figure 28.	Example of BCWS, ACWP, and BCWP all Growing at Different Linear Rates.	182
Figure 29.	Cost and Schedule Variance.	184
Figure 30.	Cost and Schedule Overruns.	185
Figure 31.	Work to be Performed, Cost to be Expended, and Work to be Scheduled.	186
Figure 32.	Decomposition of Total Program Cost into Work Packages.	188
Figure 33.	Two Options for Labeling Market Share: High – Low and Low – High.	194
Figure 34.	Notional BGC Matrix.	195
Figure 35.	Interpretation of the BCG Matrix.	195
Figure 36.	GE / McKinsey 3 x 3 Matrix.	198
Figure 37.	How the GE / McKinsey matrix is Used.	199
Figure 36.	Historical Stock Price for Weight Watchers (WTW).	202

List of Tables

Table 1.	The Ten Largest Stock Markets.	11
Table 2.	The Ten Largest Companies.	12
Table 3.	Aerospace and Defense Companies By Revenue.	13
Table 4.	Aerospace and Defense Companies by Market Capitalization.	13
Table 5.	Summary of the Boeing Annual Report.	14
Table 6.	Summary of the Lockheed-Martin Annual Report.	15
Table 7.	Summary of the BAE Systems Annual Report.	16
Table 8.	Summary of the Airbus Group Annual Report.	16
Table 9.	Summary of Direct – Indirect & Fixed – Variable Costs.	30
Table 10.	Example Pricing Methodology	38
Table 11.	2017 – 2018 NBA Rookie Salary.	42
Table 12.	The Highest Paid Athletes in the World.	43
Table 13.	Simple Example of Different Business Models	44
Table 14.	Concerns and Metrics Change as you Move up in the Organization.	69
Table 15.	The Contents of the US Code.	76
Table 16.	The Contents of the US Code of Federal Regulations.	77
Table 17.	Chapter 1 – Federal Acquisition Regulation.	83
Table 18.	Chapter 1 – Federal Acquisition Regulation Continued	84
Table 19.	The US Government Budget for 2017.	96
Table 20.	Gross Domestic Product (GDP) for 2014.	108

Table 21.	Military Expenditures for 2014.	109
Table 22.	International Traffic in Arms Regulations (ITAR)	111
Table 23.	Part 121 – United States Munitions List (USML).	112
Table 24.	Part 123 – Defense Article Licenses.	114
Table 25.	EAR Export Categories.	119
Table 26.	EAR Export Groups.	119
Table 27.	Technology Readiness Levels.	134
Table 28.	Manufacturing Readiness Levels.	135
Table 29.	Example RoI and NPV.	141
Table 30.	Rate of Return.	143
Table 31.	The Five Process Groups.	148
Table 32.	The Ten Knowledge Areas.	150
Table 33.	Key Project Management Artifacts	151
Table 34.	Example Aircraft WBS from US MIL-STD-881C,	153
Table 35.	Example Risk Register.	168
Table 36.	Examples of Institutional Investors	201
Table 37.	Title 14 – Aeronautics and Space	206
Table 38.	Title 14 Subchapter C – Aircraft.	207

ACKNOWLEDGMENTS

We gratefully acknowledge the helpful feedback provided by the following reviewers

- Ed Ashford, PhD
- Clayton Brown, LTC, US Army (ret.)
- David Edwards, PhD
- Ron Lukins, MBA
- James Powell

PREFACE

This is a book I never thought I'd write. After completing a PhD in Space Physics and getting a good job in the aerospace industry, I thought I'd be happy being a nerdy rocket scientist my entire career. But as my technical skills grew, the more I came to appreciate how business skills not only complemented my technical skills but also increased the value I brought to my employer. I realized that the most respected technical professionals were the ones that could spend a week in a room full of PhDs studying very complex technical issues, and then walk into the CEOs office and explain what all that technical analysis meant to the business.

After about a decade, I had pretty much mastered the technical skills in my chosen area of expertise – I had written the first textbook on the subject and (some years later) won the only professional award in the field. The rest of my career – and I still had more years ahead of me than I had behind me (I hoped) – would likely be a repeat of things I'd already done.

I was ready for a new challenge, and I realized that I wanted to be more than a technical contributor – I wanted to be a leader. And to lead effectively I had to master the business skills. In the years since, I've managed groups of engineers, been a business development manager for the Asia-Pacific region, and a program manager for several different product lines and development efforts. I've enjoyed the transition immensely, and I have no regrets about my change in career paths.

Although I could have taken the time to get a traditional business education, I had realized years ago that I learn best by trying to explain things to others. I also realized that I couldn't find any books or courses targeted at people like me – technical professionals who wanted to broaden their skills. Of course, there was a lot of material available on management and leadership, but a lot of it was focused on how to manage people. As a result, I decided I'd create my own course of study. One intended to help engineers – or anybody with a technical background – understand, and appreciate, the business side of the engineering profession.

To make sure I wasn't missing anything subtle, I worked with friends and colleagues who had a traditional business education. With the help of one of my friends, who has an MBA in International Marketing, I think we came up with a pretty good product.

If you're still reading this preface you're probably convinced that this kind of material will be of value to you in your career. But just in case you're still a little skeptical, let's agree that business and engineering go hand in hand. Whether you're the employee of a for profit business, or a government employee that works with employees of those businesses, this book is intended to make you more successful as an engineer – because you will have a deeper and broader understanding of how companies do business.

Let's define science to be the study of the laws of nature, and engineering to be the application of science. Similarly, let's define economics to be the study of the transfer of wealth, and business to be the application of economics.

How would you complete the following sentence?

> *Engineering is the application of science to develop new products or services that are ...*

Similarly, how would you complete the following?

> *Business is the application of economics to develop new products or services that are ...*

My answer – engineering is the application of science to develop new products or services that are "useful"; business is the application of economics to develop new products or services that are "profitable".

What happens to products that are useful, but not profitable?

The product may be of interest to a great many people, but if the business providing it is not profitable, the business will lose money and, barring financial subsidies, will go out of business – so the product will disappear from the market.

What happens to products that are profitable, but not useful?

The product may generate world class profits, but if the product is not useful – if it does not add value to the buyer – no one will buy it, so again the product will disappear from the market.

Engineering and business, go hand in hand. To be truly successful, engineers must develop products that are both useful AND profitable.

This book will help anyone with a technical background appreciate the business aspect to the project you are supporting. Even if you work for a "not for profit" business, any project you will be assigned to will have a budget and schedule. Exceed the budget and the business must cut other projects to pay for the overrun. Fall past due on the schedule, and the business will have to find a way to make up the lost time – maybe by cutting other projects. No matter how you look at it, there is always a business aspect to any engineering project.

This book is organized as follows. The *Introduction* will define some of the basic principles and set the stage for what follows. In this chapter we will review some of the earliest foundations of economics, the three factors of production, and we'll see how those three are easier to appreciate if we introduce a fourth factor – the entrepreneur. Finally, we will define the concept of a market – a place where goods are exchanged – and we will see how that has evolved into the modern-day stock market.

In the second chapter, *The Business of Business*, we will explain the importance of the stock market, (the ultimate judge of most publicly traded, for profit companies), as well as some accounting basics. We'll explore the difference between financial accounting, which is externally focused and helps create the balance sheet that measures how profitable (or not) the company is, and cost accounting, which is internally focused and helps company management understand what each product or service truly costs. We'll then explore pricing – how a company determines what it should charge for each product or service. As we will see, price is intimately related to value, so we will finish up with a discussion of value propositions and the specific business model for the products and services brought to market.

The third chapter, *Navigating the Corporation*, will clarify what the various types of non-engineers do in a large company. We will explain both what they do, and why it's important, so that you will know when you need to seek them out for their input. We will also discuss the organizational hierarchy and what changes as you move up the food chain. First and foremost, you need to learn how to tailor your message. When you're an engineer your boss is probably another engineer and will have a need to understand the technical details of what you're doing and why it's the right approach. But as you move up the organization, leadership is more interested in whether you are executing the business plan successfully, and less about the technical details of how you're doing it. We'll show you how to tailor your message based on the priorities of the different levels of the organization.

Next, we will look at *The Rules of the Road* – the laws, regulations, and guidelines that governments insist that businesses follow. Because most of our work experience is in the US, and the US economy is the largest in the world, we will be intentionally biased towards US ways of doing business. We will explore the US Federal Acquisition Regulation (FAR) that guides how the US Government conducts business and will see how that influences companies that do a lot of business with the US Government.

In the chapter on *Globalization*, we will then explore how things change when you choose to work internationally, and help you understand how you must navigate the export laws in your country of origin, as well as the import laws in the country of destination. We'll also make it clear how current exchange rates, and cultural differences, complicate the business model when you choose to cross international borders.

In the next chapter, *Planning for Success*, we will understand how to take an idea from concept to a finished product that is ready to generate sales. In short, we'll develop an appreciation for what those people in business development and program management really do (and why they should get paid if they do it well). We'll make sure to examine this from two perspectives – first for those people who work for large engineering firms, then for those entrepreneurs who are ready to strike out on their own and try to bring a new product to the market.

In the final chapter, *Evaluating Success,* we will review some of the metrics that are used to measure the business success of products or services, and we'll finish up with a detailed section on how to develop and present a business case for a new idea that will gather support from investors.

Any individual with a technical background who takes these ideas to heart is sure to become a more valuable employee – simply by being able to better relate to the non-technical people in your business. At the same time, there's also a good chance that this introduction may inspire you to start taking ownership of your project, to treat it like a business – even better, to treat it like your business (which it is) – and look past the inherently cool technical details into the necessary, and equally cool, business details.

Before we move on, some people – usually non-technical – ask about the subtitle

*How I Overcame My Moment of Inertia
and Embraced the Dark Side*

I've noticed over the years that many engineers, without any prompting from me, jokingly refer to business as "the dark side". I'll go with the flow on that one, but there's nothing dark or sinister about wanting to be part of a viable business. Once you make the leap, you'll find it's actually quite lovely on the other side of the fence.

Alan Tribble

CHAPTER 1

INTRODUCTION

This chapter will introduce some of the basic concepts and terms encountered in the field of economics. We do this to make sure we have a self-consistent base to build upon in later sections.

THE FOUR FACTORS OF PRODUCTION

The publication of Adam Smith's, *The Wealth of Nations*, in 1776 is often cited as the birth of economics as a separate discipline. Smith identified land, labor, and capital as the three factors of production, and contributors to a nation's wealth. Modern economics would add a fourth factor – the entrepreneur.

Land in this context refers to any resources that are used to create a product or service. This could be the natural resources such as water, oil, minerals, wood, etc., or it could be the components or subassemblies that are made from those natural resources. Lower tier manufacturers may harvest natural resources directly from the Earth and process them into raw materials that are easier for higher tier manufacturers to work with directly. Manufacturers of Field Programmable Gate Arrays, for example, would typically purchase refined Silicon from the mining company. The FPGA manufacturer would sell their components, FPGAs, to higher tier manufacturers that would include their FPGAs into electronic systems, and so on.

Labor refers to the activities required to process the resources (land) from the raw material you start with, into the finished product. For the mining company in the previous paragraph, this would include the physical effort of the miners who pull Silicon from the ground. For the FPGA manufacturer, this would include the physical effort of the workers who process the refined Silicon into the FPGAs.

Capital refers to wealth, specifically money or other assets (e.g., equipment that can assist with design, manufacturing, or test). Money is equivalent to equipment, because if you don't have the right equipment you can purchase it with cash. If you purchase the right equipment you may be able to reduce your labor costs.

By the way, capitalism refers to the creation of goods and services for profit, in an economic system based on private ownership of the means of production.

The fourth and final factor in production is the entrepreneur – the individual who figures out a way to combine land, labor, and capital in a new manner to fill a need. Without the entrepreneur, the driving force behind a vision, new products would rarely come to market.

How does the entrepreneur do it? In some cases, they develop a new concept, a new product or service that has value in the eyes of the buyer and create a new market. In other cases, they may simply streamline the other three factors of production. If the entrepreneur can find a way to create raw materials more cheaply, then our costs would go down and we could either: i) increase our profits; or ii) reduce the price of our product and make it more affordable, and maybe make it appeal to more buyers. If more people could buy it the market would grow. Similarly, if the entrepreneur can find a way to obtain the labor required more cheaply, but making the work force more productive, then we can produce more products in less time, which would reduce their cost. Of course, another way to reduce the labor cost might be to move the location of the factory to a part of the world where people are willing to work for less.

That last thought leads to a couple of questions about the cost of the laborers in your work force.

> How can high paid domestic workers compete against low paid foreign workers who earn half as much or less?

and while we're at it

> How can high paid senior workers compete against low paid junior workers who earn half as much or less?

The answer – by being more productive. Consider the following:

Why Brooks Brothers is Investing in Veteran Tailors[1]

At a pioneering plant in New York, half the workers are older than 55

Yeje and her peers can cost more to employ than their younger colleagues. Older sewers in the alterations department—where half the factory's employees work, altering about 225,000 items of clothing a year from stores with too much work to handle—can earn up to 15 percent more in pay than newbies. But Brooks Brothers considers the veterans a worthwhile investment, because they excel at speed and precision and make few mistakes. The operation is largely automated, but some work is still done by hand, and older, more experienced tailors are more skilled. They can make sample neckties in only 30 minutes—a task a newbie can't handle. Twenty minutes later those ties are in the hands of Brooks Brothers executives at headquarters in Manhattan.

---

[1] http://www.bloomberg.com/news/articles/2016-03-09/where-retirement-isn-t-job-one

Just remember, as long as cost is a significant criterion, if you can get more work done per unit cost than the next person you will be in demand. If their ratio of work per unit cost is equal to or greater than yours, you may have trouble finding a position that will pay you what you want to get paid.

The third and final way the entrepreneur could streamline the means of production is to increase the amount of capital on hand. As we saw, in this context capital (or cash) can be used to purchase more equipment. If the entrepreneur can increase the amount of available equipment, then we could process more product in less time, with greater accuracy, and so on. Cash on hand means you can buy equipment quickly. More cash on hand creates options, and less cash on hand restricts options. (As we'll see in the section on cost accounting, equipment is often "capitalized" for tax purposes, but more on that later.)

Although there are certainly a number of wealthy entrepreneurs that can bring new ideas to market without assistance, there are also a lot of entrepreneurs in the making – people who have great ideas but not quite enough cash available to make them a reality. What happens when you have a great idea, but not enough cash to bring it to market? You look for people willing to lend you money. Small entrepreneurs may borrow from Mom and Dad. Lucky entrepreneurs may go on television shows such as *The Shark Tank*™ or *The Profit*™ or find a venture capitalist willing to invest. Large businesses borrow money by selling shares in the stock market.

We have used the term "market" a few times, but we haven't really defined it yet. We'll explore the different types of markets in the next section.

FREE AND CONTROLLED MARKETS

As the name implies, when we use the term "market" feel free to imagine what we today might call a "farmers market", only transport yourself back several hundred years and imagine the business of the marketplace without the advantages of modern transportation, or communications. Buyers would go to the market because they had a need – a need to acquire some good or service – and sellers would go to the market because they also had a need – in this case a need to sell some good or service or trade it for something else. In short, a market is a place – either physical or virtual – where buyers and sellers meet to conduct business. Today the term market is almost interchangeable in some contexts with "customer". When you ask – what is the market for your product? You're really asking –what type of people or organizations would buy it?

This last point may see obvious, but it's very important to understand the difference between the "global" market and your "addressed" market. We used to work with a great engineer who was always bubbling over with good ideas, but his business case always boiled down to

The population of the world is Y, and if X% of the world buys my product, I'll be fabulously wealthy.

No disagreement with that overly simplistic math, but he would have done a lot better job presenting his business case if he would have focused on what portion of the world he was really trying to reach and shown data to support his guess as to what percentage of the addressed market would really buy his product, and why.

In any market, both buyers and sellers have a choice. In times of plenty, a buyer who wants to purchase goods may find an abundance of suppliers, all of whom are eager to earn his or her business. Given many choices, the buyer would naturally look for the best bargain, as judged by some combination of price, quality, and quantity. Realizing that the buyer has many options, sellers who would rather make some sale (and reap some profit) rather than nothing at all, would be inclined to drop prices. This is what we would call a "buyer's market". In times of shortage, there may be few if any sellers, offering the goods desired. As a result, buyers would be willing to pay more to acquire the goods they need rather than go home empty handed. Of course, this would be a seller's market.

Two other terms used to describe a market are "free" and "controlled". The buyers and sellers markets we just described are consequences of a free market. In a free market, product availability and prices are driven by the law of supply and demand. That is, prices reflect consumer habits, and competition. Over the short term, prices may go up or down depending on whether it's a sellers' market or buyers' market. But over the long term, prices will tend to decrease, and quality will tend to increase, as sellers compete for market share. This is because customers will always try to obtain goods or services in the place where they are cheapest (i.e., the best value).

The alternative to a free market is a controlled market. In a controlled market prices are set arbitrarily – often by the Government – and are not affected by the law of supply and demand. In a controlled market there is little motivation manufacturers to reduce cost, or add value, since the price is set independently. Conversely, in a free market competition should flourish because other entrepreneurs are always trying to find a way to improve upon existing products or services, so they can increase their share of the market.

The stock market is a specific example of a free market. The two biggest stock exchanges in the United States are the New York Stock Exchange, founded in 1792, and the NASDAQ, founded in 1971. It is a place where people meet to buy and sell "shares" of stock. What is stock? Partial ownership in a company. They are called shares because each piece of stock is entitled to a proportional share of the company's profit or loss. Selling shares of stock is how publicly traded companies borrow money. Buying shares of stock is (hopefully) how buyers increase their wealth. People who buy shares of stock today, typically do so because they believe the share of stock will be more valuable in the future, so they could sell it at a profit. Publicly traded companies increase the wealth of the shareholders by increasing the value of their shares.

We'll examine stock markets in more detail in the next chapter, *The Business of Business*. Just remember that shareholders buy stock because they expect them to go up in value, at a greater rate than other investment opportunities. Shareholders sell stock because they either need some short-term cash or believe there are other investments that will offer a greater long term financial return. As we'll see in the chapter on *Evaluating Success* much of the challenge of running a successful business is keeping the shareholders happy.

Finally, never forget that, in general, free markets are amoral. They reward scarcity, not intrinsic value. They provide products we <u>want </u>to buy, not just those that we <u>need</u>.

For additional information see *Naked Economics: Undressing the Dismal Science*, by Charles Wheelan.

CHAPTER 2

THE BUSINESS OF BUSINESS

Before we jump into the details, let's ask a basic question.

What is the difference between the business of "*insert the name of the company you work for or industry you work in*" and the business of "business"?

In general, business is about delivering products and services that meet the needs of our customers. The business of business is – and this sounds cynical because it is – about advancing the wealth of the shareholders. At this point we could have a great philosophical discussion to debate – is that really what it's all about, advancing the wealth of the shareholders?

Although we think there's much more to life than just that, we think this is the price of admission in a capitalistic society. You have to make money to stay in business, because money is what funds your new product development activities, and new products and services are what keep your customers coming back for more.

Although there are some exceptions to the rule, (for Government agencies and certain non-profit organizations), in general – if you can't turn a profit, you will go out of business.

Having said that, the best companies look at profit as one metric of success, not just the metric of success. Many of us choose the industry we work in, (such as aerospace and defense, health care, or telecommunications), because we like those products. Aeronautical engineers like seeing aircraft that they helped design fly faster and farther than any other aircraft before. Astronautical engineers like seeing the launch vehicle that they helped build send satellites to other planets. This gives us a great feeling of accomplishment.

While we admit that a business has to be profitable, we would also say that you have to have a higher purpose. Without one, you will lose your focus, and when you lose focus you lose business.

STOCK MARKETS

There are over 100 stock markets around the world, trading stock in thousands of different publicly traded companies. The ten largest stock exchanges in the world, as judged by the value of the stocks they trade, are shown in Table 1.

Over 22,000 stocks – valued at over $35 trillion US Dollars – are traded on those ten exchanges alone. Several of the largest companies in the world are traded on more than one exchange, as shown in Table 2

Before we move on, let's define a couple of terms. Market capitalization is the total dollar value of all the company's outstanding shares. Simplistically, it's the price of a single share of stock multiplied by the number of shares issued.

When your stock broker tells you to invest in "large", "mid", or "small" cap stocks she is recommending companies that have a market capitalization as shown below:

- Large Cap: $10 billion plus
- Mid Cap: $2 billion to $10 billion
- Small Cap: Less than $2 billion
    - Micro Cap: $50M to $2B
    - Nano cap: < $50M

Table 1. The Ten Largest Stock Markets.
(Source – https://www.stockmarketclock.com/exchanges)

Rank	Stock Exchange	Symbol	Country	Market Capitalization ($B US)
1	New York Stock Exchange	NYSE	United States	$ 19,600
2	National Association of Security Dealers Automated Quotations	NASDAQ	United States	$ 8,130
3	London Stock Exchange	LSE	United Kingdom	$ 5,120
4	Tokyo Stock Exchange	JPX	Japan	$ 4,270
5	Shanghai Stock Exchange	SSE	China	$ 3,610
6	Hong Kong Stock Exchange	HKEX	China	$ 3,490
7	Euronext Amsterdam Stock Exchange	Euronext	European Union	$ 3,370
8	Toronto Stock Exchange	TSX	Canada	$ 3,240
9	Shenzhen Stock Exchange	SZSE	China	$ 2,070
10	Frankfurt Stock Exchange	FSX	Germany	$ 1,770

Table 2. The Ten Largest Companies.
(Source - http://fortune.com/global500/)

Rank	Company	Exchange	Revenue ($B)
1	Walmart	NYSE	$ 485.9
2	State Grid Corp	NA - Private	$ 315.2
3	Sinopec Group	HKEX, LSE, NYSE, SSE	$ 267.5
4	China National Petroleum	NA - Private	$ 262.6
5	Toyota Motor	LSE, NYSE, TYO	$ 254.7
6	Volkswagen	FSE	$ 240.3
7	Royal Dutch Shell	Euronext, LSE, NYSE	$ 240.0
8	Berkshire Hathaway	NYSE	$ 223.6
9	Apple	NASDAQ	$ 215.6
10	Exxon Mobil	NYSE	$ 205.0

It's hard to compare retail companies like Walmart in the United States with petroleum giants like Sinopec in China, so let's do a comparison within a single industry. Consider the largest aerospace and defense companies, as measured by sales, Table 3, and market capitalization, Table 4. As can easily be seen, 7 of the 10 companies – all of which happen to be based in the US – are traded on the New York Stock Exchange (NYSE). The 3 other companies are based in Europe with Airbus and Leonardo (formerly Finmeccanica) reporting sales in Euros, and British Aerospace reporting results in Pounds.

Although these companies are all in the same industry – aerospace and defense – how would we judge whether a single share of Lockheed-Martin, the stock in Table 3 with the highest revenue, is a better deal than Boeing, the stock in Table 4 with the highest market capitalization?

Table 3. Aerospace and Defense Companies by Revenue.
(Source – http://people.defensenews.com/top-100/)

Rank	Company	Country	Revenue ($M)
1	Lockheed-Martin	United States	$ 43,468
2	Boeing	United States	$ 29,500
3	BAE Systems	United Kingdom	$ 23,622
4	Raytheon	United States	$ 22,384
5	Northrop-Grumman	United States	$ 20,200
6	General Dynamics	United States	$ 19,696
7	Airbus	France / Netherlands	$ 12,321
8	L3 Technologies	United States	$ 8,879
9	Leonardo	Italy	$ 8,526
10	Thales	France	$ 8,362

Table 4. Aerospace and Defense Companies by Market Capitalization.
(Source – https://gfmasset.com/2017/01/40-largest-aerospace-defense-stocks-by-market-cap-2017/)

Rank	Company	Country	Market Cap ($M)
1	Boeing	United States	$ 96,877
2	United Technologies	United States	$ 91,316
3	Lockheed-Martin	United States	$ 74,413
4	General Dynamics	United States	$ 53,455
5	Airbus Group	Netherlands	$ 51,501
6	Raytheon	United States	$ 43,072
7	Northrop Grumman	United States	$ 41,466
8	Safran SA	France	$ 30,065
9	BAE Systems	United Kingdom	$ 23,084
10	Thales SA	France	$ 20,139

To answer that question, we'd have to dig deeper than the stock price itself and appreciate some of the factors that investors used when they determine the value of the stock. Those factors are almost always found in the company's annual report – a document that the company's management provides to the shareholders that explains what happened during the past year and why they should (or shouldn't) be optimistic about the company's future.

Let's compare the annual report for two US companies – Lockheed-Martin and Boeing, as shown in Table 5 and Table 6, respectively. The first thing that jumps out is that not a single line item on either report seems to map one to one.

Why aren't they standardized? Because there's no legal requirement that they follow the same format. As a result, each company can choose a format that they think will appeal to their shareholders and also convey the information they want to highlight.

Is it any different if we compare two European companies? Let's look at the BAE Systems and Airbus Group reports, as shown in Table 7 and Table 8, respectively. Again, no single line item – other than dividends per share – is the same. Still some common terms arise when you compare all the reports together. There is a consistent use of terms like – orders; sales; income; earnings; dividends; assets; debt; margin and so on. In order to understand how these terms are used, we need to understand some basic accounting principles. More specifically, we need to understand the financial accounting (or general accounting) principles that come into play when companies report their financial performance to their shareholders.

Table 5. Summary of the Boeing Annual Report.

In $ millions, except per share data	2016	2015	2014
Revenues	94,751	96,114	90,762
Core operating earnings	5,464	7,741	8,860
Core operating margins	5.80%	8.10%	9.80%
Core earnings per share	7.24	7.72	8.6
Operating cash flow	10,499	9,363	8,858
Contractual Backlog	458,272	476,595	487,092
Total Backlog	473,492	489,299	502,291

Table 6. Summary of the Lockheed-Martin Annual Report.

In $ millions, except per share data	2016	2015	2014
Net Sales	47,248	40,536	39,946
Segment Operating Profit	5,100	4,978	5,116
Consolidated Operating Profit	5,549	4,712	5,012
Net Earnings From Continuing Operations	3,753	3,126	3,253
Net Earnings	5,302	3,605	3,614
Diluted Earnings per Common Share			
Continuing Operations	12.38	9.93	10.09
Net Earnings	17.49	11.46	11.21
Cash Dividends per Common Share	6.77	6.15	5.49
Average Diluted Common Shares Outstanding	303	315	322
Cash and Cash Equivalents	1,837	1,090	1,446
Total Assets	47,806	49,304	37,190
Total Debt	14,282	15,261	6,142
Stockholders' Equity	1,606	3,097	3,400
Common Shares Outstanding at Year End	289	303	314
Net Cash Provided by Operating Activities	5,189	5,101	3,866

Table 7. Summary of the BAE Systems Annual Report.

In £ millions, except per share data	2016	2015	2014
Sales	19,020	17,904	16,637
Underlying EBITA	1,905	1,683	1,702
Order Backlog	42,000		40,500
Operating Profit	1,742	1,502	1,300
Operating Business Cash Flow	1,004	681	1,191
Net Debt	-1,542	-1,422	-1,032
Underlying Earnings per Share	40.3p	40.2p	38.0p
Basic Earnings per Share	28.8p	29.0p	23.4p
Dividends per Share			20.5p

Table 8. Summary of the Airbus Group Annual Report.

In € billions, except per share data	2016	2015	2014
Order intake	134.5	159	166.4
Order book	1,060	1,005.90	857.5
Revenue	66.6	64.5	60.7
EBIT	2.3	4.1	4
Net Income	0.995	2.7	2.3
Net Cash Position	11.1	10	9.1
R&D Expenses	3	3.5	3.4
Earnings per Share	1.29	3.43	2.99
Dividends per Share	1.35	1.3	1.22

FINANCIAL ACCOUNTING

What determines when a business is successful? For that matter, who makes the determination? Is it the shareholders, the customers, the employees?

The answers would of course vary depending on who you ask, but one metric that most would agree on is profitability. As we noted earlier, businesses that are trying to deliver a product to a well-defined market, but cannot do so at a profit, have a tendency to go out of business. In this chapter we will examine some of the basic concepts that are used to measure a business's financial performance. Let's begin with a few definitions.

Order

A request for an item.

The plural of order, orders, is often used and is simply the total of the individual orders.

Sale

The exchange of an item for money.

The plural of sale, sales, is often used and is simply the total amount of money the business received from providing goods or services.

The distinction between orders and sales may seem subtle, but it's important. It's easy to see the difference when you take the example of eating out at a restaurant. First, you place your order for the food you want by making a request of the server. Later, after receiving the food and confirming it really was what you ordered, and was of sufficient quality, you pay for it. That is the sale. Orders precede sales. In the restaurant business, there may be only a few minutes between the order and the sale. In the aerospace and defense industry, it could be months or years between the order and the sale. The lead time for a large aircraft like the Boeing 747 or Airbus A380 aircraft approaches 24 months for example. Because there can be many months between the order and the sale in some industries, comparing sales and orders can be a rough indication of whether the company is growing or shrinking. If orders exceed sales, it is an indication that the company is building a backlog of products to be delivered (or conversely, that it's having issues in its manufacturing process). If sales exceed orders, it's an indication that its backlog is shrinking.

Another important term is:

Expenses

The amount of money it cost the business to provide the goods or services.

The most basic accounting relation is

$$Profit\ (or\ Loss) = Sales - Expenses$$

If sales exceed expenses, the business has positive cash flow and is generating a profit. If expenses exceed sales, the business has negative cash flow and is operating at a loss.

We note that there are only two ways to increase profits – increase sales or decrease expenses. Which of those two options you choose to emphasize is critically important and will affect the future of the business. Most companies proactively try to do both.

As we will see in more detail in the chapter on *The Rules of the Road*, businesses must pay taxes and convince their shareholders that they are a growing viable business. Of course, there's a legal, truthful way to do this that is and most businesses around the world follow the International Financial Reporting Standards (IFRS). Historically, the US has followed a different standard known as the Generally

Accepted Accounting Principles (GAAP). The differences between the GAAP and IFRS may seem subtle to non-accounting professionals, but in general GAAP is "rule based" whereas IFRS is "principle based". IFRS often allows more flexibility than GAAP. The US has agreed to move the GAAP toward the IFRS, but just remember that the IFRS and GAAP provide a framework for reporting results, but don't mandate a single correct methodology. As such, the specific practices of any individual business will probably be a little different than the general example that follows.

As we just saw, sales minus expenses equals profit. Sales come from your customers, and profit – if not reinvested in the business – would go to the owners. Between sales and profit are several intermediate measures of financial performance as shown in Figure 1.

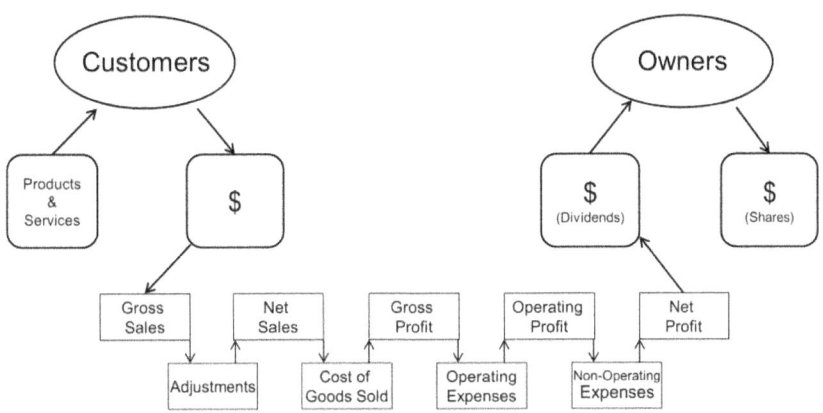

Figure 1. Sales, Profit, and Other Measures of Financial Performance.

Gross Sales

This is the simple total of all sales invoices. Quite simply it is the number of items sold multiplied by manufacturer's suggested retail price (also known as the list price). Gross sales are usually more important for the consumer retail industry than higher tech industries. For example, most airlines can negotiate better deals for a fleet of aircraft, as opposed to paying the list price for a single aircraft. (FYI, Airbus reports a 2018 average list price of $445.6M for an A380.) Still Gross Sales is a rough measure of the amount of product sold.

Adjustments

Adjustments to gross sales are made for

i) Returns – when customers return defective or damaged products, and get their money back;

ii) Allowances - when customers agree to keep damaged merchandise for a reduction in the selling price; or

iii) Discounts – a reduced price offered for paying in cash, or within a certain amount of time.

These adjustments are more often used in lower technology consumer industries, as opposed to higher tech industries like aerospace and defense. Subtracting adjustments from gross sales gives net sales.

Net Sales = Gross Sales – Adjustments

Net sales are a better measure of the actual cash generated by the business. On the income statement "sales" values refer to net sales, not gross sales. Net sales are also referred to as "revenue".

Cost of Goods Sold

This includes all the costs associated with producing the goods that are sold, such as material (land), labor, and allocated overhead expenses. The costs of goods built, but not yet sold, are treated separately as inventory.

Subtracting the cost of goods sold from net sales gives gross profit.

$$\text{Gross Profit} = \text{Net Sales} - \text{Cost of Goods Sold}$$

Gross profit is also known as sales profit. It is a rough measure of how profitable a business is but has not yet accounted for all other expenses associated with doing business, such as operating expenses.

Operating Expenses

This includes other expenses incurred in carrying out a business' day-to-day activities, but not directly associated with production, such as General and Administrative (G&A) expenses – which may include: Rent, Utilities, Employee Benefits, Managerial Salaries, Travel, Research & Development (R&D), Bid & Proposal (B&P), …; as well as Selling expenses – Commissions, Advertising, …

Subtracting operating expenses from gross profit gives operating profit.

$$\text{Operating Profit} = \text{Gross Profit} - \text{Operating Expenses}$$

Operating profit reflects the profit after all expenses are included, but does not yet include non-operating expenses such as interest, taxes, depreciation, etc. Operating profit is also known as Earnings Before Interest, Taxes, Depreciation, and Amortization (EBITDA). Related terms are Earnings Before Interest and Taxes; Earnings Before Taxes, aka Profit Before Tax (PBT); and Earnings After Taxes, aka Profit After Tax (PAT).

Non-Operating Expenses

As we just saw, non-operating expenses include things like interest and taxes. It also includes capital expenses – onetime expenses to acquire or upgrade physical assets with multi-year lifetimes. This may include facilities, test equipment, and so on. These expenses can be amortized or "depreciated" over many years, so are addressed separately.

Depreciation is the systematic reduction in the cost of fixed assets, such as buildings, equipment, and so on. (An exception is land, which is not depreciated since its value does not decrease over time.) Depreciation of assets is a method of matching the cost of an asset to the revenue that it generates. For example, if you buy a piece of test equipment and you expect it to remain in service for five years before you have to replace it with newer technology, then you would want to depreciate its costs to each of the five years it will be in service. This gives you the chance to compare the annual cost of the asset to the revenue it helps generate, each year. The general rule is that if the useful life of the asset is longer than the taxable year, then the cost must be depreciated.

Subtracting non-operating expenses from operating profit leaves net profit.

> *Net Profit = Operating Profit*
> *– Non-Operating Expenses*

Net profit is the amount of money left after paying for all expenses. This is the money that the company could return to its shareholders as dividends, reinvest in expanding the business, or save for future needs.

One other term commonly seen in financial analysis is margin. Simply put, margin is a measure of the difference between profit and sales. Gross, operating, and net profits all have corresponding margins:

> *Gross Margin = Gross Profit – Net Sales*
>
> *Operating Margin = Operating Profit – Net Sales*
>
> *Net Margin = Net Profit – Net Sales*

Margins are a typical means of measuring the profitability of a company or product line. Higher margins mean higher profits. Net margin is also known as Return on Sales (ROS).

A brief aside here, but if you ever watch a television shown like the *Shark Tank™* or *The Profit™*, you will notice that the people evaluating the business ideas are always concerned with the margin. Simply speaking, margin is a measure of how easy it will be to generate a profit. A product with a high margin – a high difference between what it costs to produce and what it can be sold for – can become profitable much more easily than a product with a low margin – a low difference between what it costs to produce and what it can be sold for. In some cases, the market place only has room for low margin products. But if the margin is higher, the chance of higher profits goes up dramatically.

While we're at it, we should also define a couple of other terms often seen in literature describing a company's financial performance.

Assets

Assets are things that have value. Having value means they are likely to result in future economic benefit. Assets include cash on hand, as well as accounts receivable – money owed to us by a customer, and also capital equipment – which could be sold to generate cash. Intellectual Property, such as patents and trademarks, or even trade secrets, are also valuable. The term "liquidity" is used to describe the ease with which a business can convert its assets to cash.

Liabilities

Liabilities are legal commitments to pay off debt. This may include notes payable – money we owe to a bank, accounts payable – money we owe a supplier, and so on.

It's important to note that sometimes the same item may have characteristics of both an asset and a liability. If you sign a contract to purchase a new house, or a new car, but you still own money on the loan – is it an asset or a liability? It's an asset in that it has intrinsic value, you could – at least in theory – sell it for cash. At the same time, because you still owe money on the loan, it's also a liability.

The difference between assets and liabilities is another basic accounting relation

Equity = Assets – Liabilities

If the equity is positive the business (or item) could – at least in theory – be sold off to settle all of its debts and leave the owners with money left over. If the equity is negative, selling off all the assets would not be enough to cover all the debts, leaving the owners with a stack of bills they would still have an obligation to pay.

As we just saw, margins were a convenient way of comparing profits to expenses. Similarly, ratios are a convenient way of comparing assets to liabilities. Two useful ratios are

Current Ratio = Assets / Liabilities

Quick Ratio = (Cash + Accounts Receivable) / Liabilities

Quick in this context means quickly converted to cash. Ratios will vary widely across firms and industries, but the higher the better. Just remember that margins and ratios are shortcuts that allow observers to collapse the gory details in a balance sheet down to a few simple numbers. They are sometimes useful for investors – but they never tell the whole story. They are indicators of financial performance, and not the final answer.

DISCRETIONARY SPENDING

It seems obvious that customers, given a choice, would rather pay less for the products and services they buy. If the expenses a company has are fixed, lower sales would naturally translate into lower profit. Unfortunately, the company owners – the shareholders – would prefer the opposite. Owners would prefer higher profits, which are easier to generate with higher selling prices. As shown in Figure 2, it's a delicate balancing act. Discretionary spending – the spending that is not fixed, or mandatory, but optional – is the tool used to achieve balance. Different types of discretionary, and non-discretionary, expenses are shown in Figure 3.

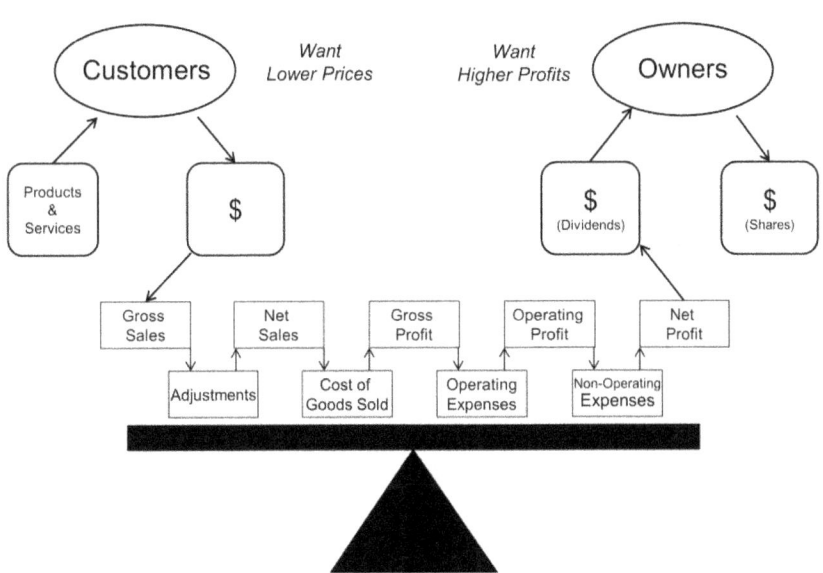

Figure 2. Balancing the Needs of Customers and Owners.

It's generally accepted in many industries that allowing customers to make returns is better for business in the long term. Customers don't get mad because they got stuck with something they didn't want and take their business elsewhere. In some cases, returning some items is simply not allowed by law. For example, you can't return unused medication to the pharmacy for a refund. For that reason, we tend to think of returns as a non-discretionary expense, because the company has no real say in determining what gets returned. We would term the other adjustments – allowances and discounts – as discretionary expenses because the company does get to decide what discount they will approve, or what allowance they will make.

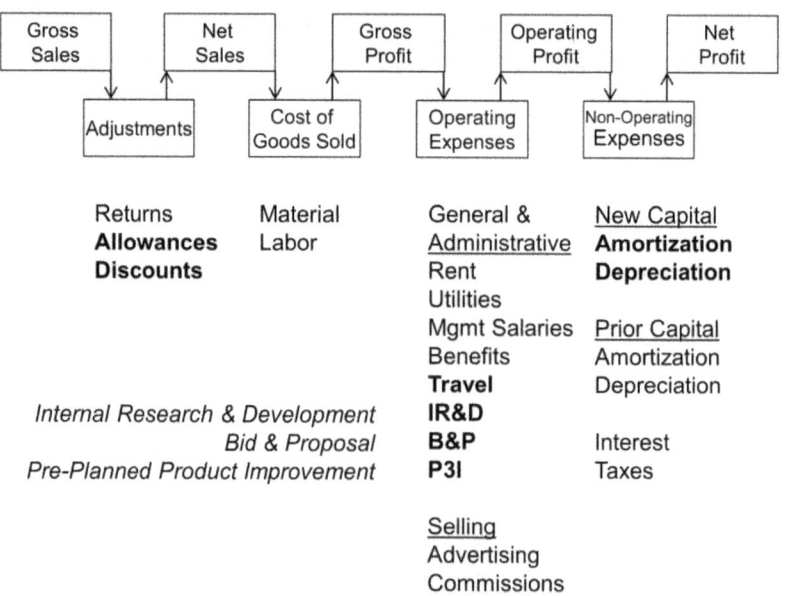

Figure 3. Examples of Discretionary Expenses.

Moving to the cost of goods sold column, we think of material and labor expenses as being fixed or non-discretionary. The company agrees on a purchase price for its material, and a wage for its workers, up front. If business conditions change the company may be able to negotiate a better deal, or be forced to make concessions, but these values – once set – typically don't change very frequently.

Discretionary expenses start to become obvious when we get to the General & Administrative or Selling categories. Key examples of discretionary spending are the amount of money a company agrees to spend on the following:

- Internal Research & Development (IR&D)
    o The money planned for investment in new product development

- Bid & Proposals (B&P)
    o The money planned to support bids and proposals in hopes of winning new business

- Advertising
    o The money planned for ads in newspapers, magazines, or for attendance at trade shows

Because the business itself makes the decision about how much to spend on these topics they are clearly discretionary expenses. Each year, during the planning cycle, the business decides how much money they can set aside for these discretionary expenses and still keep the shareholders happy. Reinvestment in the business is a requirement, because without developing new products, putting in proposals for new business, or advertising spent to let potential customers know about your product, business will begin to drop off. At the other extreme, if you put too much money into IR&D, then some shareholders will argue that you're too focused on the long term and may choose to seek investments with better short-term growth opportunities. Adjusting the discretionary expenses to achieve the right balance is a bit of an art form, as opposed to a science.

Although a company will plan out the amount of discretionary spending it intends for each category before the start of the next accounting period, when things change it's not unusual to adjust discretionary spending in the accounting period itself. For example, if the company assumed they would win a major program early in the year, and that sales from that program would generate additional cash that could contribute to discretionary spending, they may have to cut back on spending if the program is delayed, cancelled, or lost to the competition. Cuts in discretionary spending are not unusual as business conditions change.

At the same time, it's certainly possible to increase discretionary spending, but that is often harder to do. The company owners are expecting the company to generate a predictable amount of sales and profit, all of which are predicted in the company's annual report. Cut profit expectations and the share price often suffers. An intermediate step is often to move money between discretionary spending accounts, rather than disappoint the owners. If a major pursuit crops up unexpectedly, and you want to submit a proposal but didn't have the money to do that in your plans for B&P, then you may decide to move money from IR&D into B&P and keep the total amount of discretionary spending the same.

All of this discussion about what you spend in each category of course assumes you have a good understanding of what your expenses are. The part of accounting that focuses on understanding and controlling your costs is known, appropriately, as cost accounting and is the subject of the next section.

COST ACCOUNTING

Financial accounting focuses on understanding profit and loss, (keeping score). Financial accounting is externally focused, reporting results to the investors, the government, creditors, etc.

Cost accounting focuses on understanding the costs of producing the goods or services, to enable cost control and cost reduction. Cost accounting is internally focused to support management decision making.

In one sense, keeping track of your costs should be straight forward. Simply make a list of everything you spend money on, and the total is the amount of cost you incurred. The challenge is having visibility to how much you spent on which products and services that you offered to your customers. If you can't make a reasonably accurate assessment of what it costs you to provide a product or service, you won't know how you need to price them to turn a profit. This is the ultimate objective of cost accounting – to confirm what it costs to produce the individual products and services that your business sells to customers.

Let's begin by defining some terms:

Direct Costs

These are costs that can be directly traced to the product (or service). This includes the cost of the materials that go into the product, and the cost of the labor it takes to build it and test it.

Indirect Costs

These are costs that can't be directly traced to the product. Loosely speaking this includes all "overhead" costs such as: utilities; rent; marketing; office supplies; and the labor cost of personnel who don't work directly on the individual products, such as the executives.

Two independent, but closely related terms, are:

Fixed Costs

These are costs that are static, and don't vary with the level of production, such as the lease on a building. The lease is the same regardless of whether the factory inside is running at maximum capacity or sitting idle.

Variable Costs

These are costs that vary with the level of production. This would include the material and labor used in production. If more units are produced, more materials must be purchased, and more labor hours must go into manufacturing.

As shown in Table 9, every cost can be defined as either Direct or Indirect AND Fixed or Variable.

Table 9. Summary of Direct – Indirect & Fixed – Variable Costs.

Direct / Fixed Costs	**Direct / Variable Costs**
Costs that are directly traceable to the product, and do not vary with the rate of production 　Example 　　Labor costs for a production supervisor that oversees only one product	Costs that are directly traceable to the product, but do vary with the rate of production 　Example 　　Cost of the raw materials, parts, sub-assemblies, … needed to manufacture the product 　　Labor costs for the workers that assemble the product may also be included
Indirect / Fixed Costs	**Indirect / Variable Costs**
Costs that are not directly traceable to the product, and do not vary with the rate of production 　Example 　　Depreciation on assembly or test assets used to support multiple product lines	Costs that are not directly traceable to the product, but do vary with the rate of production 　Example 　　Utility costs for assembly or test assets used to support multiple product lines

If we can list all of the costs that are directly, or indirectly, tied to completing our product (or service), and we then divide by the number of units produced, we can obtain a rough estimate of the unit cost. The mathematical relation is:

$$\text{Unit Cost} = \frac{[\text{Direct Costs} + (X\% \times \text{Indirect Costs})]}{\text{\# Units Produced}}$$

where *X%* is the fraction of the indirect costs that you choose to allocate to this product, rather than to other products.

Sometimes there is no obviously right or wrong answer, so you get to make a choice about how you allocate your indirect costs. You may choose to allocate more to one product line, and less to another. At the same time, it's not always obvious what costs are direct or indirect. In the example above, we stated that the labor costs for a production supervisor that only oversees one product was a direct / fixed cost. Direct because the cost of that supervisors' salary and benefits is spent entirely in support of that single product line, and fixed because (in most cases) the supervisor's salary is set at the beginning of the year and does not vary from month to month if production rates vary.

But what should we do if the supervisor is responsible for managing people that support more than one product line? In that case, we may choose to treat that cost as an indirect cost and allocate portions of it to each of the product lines supported. The point is, there's rarely a single right answer, and the process of allocating indirect costs to products can be as much art as science. The key is to be consistent. Once you decide how you're going to do it for one product line, do it the same way for all the other product lines.

Of course, if you're doing business with a Government, then they get to have a say in how you do your cost accounting. In the US, this is all spelled out in the US Code of Federal

Regulations, specifically in Title 48 – Federal Acquisition Regulations System, Chapter 99 – Cost Accounting Standards Board. In the discussion that follows we will over simplify the details that your favorite cost accountant probably knows by heart, so we can understand the basic principles. The specific implementation varies from industry to industry, and from company to company, but the basic concepts remain the same.

Recall that in Figure 1 one of the key topics was "Cost of Goods Sold". The challenge of cost accounting boils down to determining what costs should be mapped directly to individual products, or services, and what costs should be left as indirect costs that would be lumped into the general categories of operating expenses or non-operating expenses. This calculation is often done separately for different products, and for different types of employees, within an organization.

For example, if you're an engineer you know you get paid a salary, and you probably appreciate that the amount of money your employer charges for your time is probably 2 or 3 (or more) times what you get paid. That difference accounts for all the other direct and indirect costs, in addition to your salary and benefits, which it takes to keep you happy and efficient. Those other expenses include things like the lease on the office building you work in, the cost of your desk and chair, the cost of your computer and the Information Technology specialists that show up to fix it when it locks up, and so on.

As we can all appreciate, if you compare two software engineers selected at random, they probably won't make the same salary. That difference is, in part, driven by their experience and responsibility. Younger, less experienced engineers typically make less than older, more experienced engineers. So, one question we have to answer is – do we want to charge different rates for engineers at different levels of seniority, or are we okay charging a single rate? Either way works, but with the first approach you now have a more complicated cost structure. You must do the calculation separately for each different level of seniority in the rate structure. Do it that way and the less experienced engineers cost less than the more experienced engineers. But you could also choose to put all the engineers in the same category and charge a single rate for each.

So, if you want to calculate the true cost of a software engineer, when averaged over a year, you would simply go back to the general formula:

> Unit Cost = [Direct Costs + (X% × Indirect Costs)] / # Units Produced

and tweak it a bit to make it read

> Hourly Cost of SW Engr =
> [Direct Costs for SW Engrs +
> (X% × Indirect Costs for SW Engrs) /
> # Hours all SW Engrs worked

where again you make a conscious decision about what fraction of indirect costs, X%, you allocate to software engineers, vs everything else.

Do that same calculation as many times as you want, until you have separate rates for software, firmware, and hardware engineers, or for systems engineers and test engineers, and so on. Each of those separate categories are referred to as cost pools, activity pools, or similar terms like work centers. Do that for most employees in the company – the executives are usually kept separate from that calculation as we'll see in a minute – and we can estimate what an hour of every employees' time costs the company.

If we do a similar calculation for each product we can also figure out what they cost. If you want to calculate the true

Business Management for Engineers • 33

cost of product A you would simply go back to the general formula:

$$\text{Unit Cost} = [\text{Direct Costs} + (X\% \times \text{Indirect Costs})] / \#\text{ Units Produced}$$

and tweak it a bit to make it read

$$\text{Unit Cost of Product A} = [\text{Direct Costs for Product A} + (X\% \times \text{Indirect / Fixed Costs for Product A}) / \#\text{ Units of Product A Manufactured}$$

where again you make a conscious decision about what fraction of indirect costs you allocate to Product A, vs Products B, C, D, etc.

Again, that's rather oversimplified, but our purpose is to help you understand the basic principles, not make you an expert at cost accounting. If you need more detail, take your favorite cost accountant to lunch.

At this point, we have notionally understood how to calculate the Cost of Goods Sold (COGS), or equivalent terms such as Cost of Sales (COS). But back to Figure 1, we haven't yet figured in operating expenses or non-operating expenses. Operating expenses include

- General and Administrative (G&A) expenses
    - Rent, Utilities, Employee Benefits, Managerial Salaries, Travel, Research & Development (R&D), Bid & Proposal (B&P), ...
- Selling expenses
    - Commissions, Advertising, ...

Non-operating expenses include:

- Capital Expenses
    - One-time expenses to acquire or upgrade physical assets with multi-year lifetimes, because these expenses can be amortized or depreciated. (This includes facilities, test equipment, ...)

- Interest

- Taxes

It is standard practice to account for the additional operating expenses by calculating the General & Administrative (G&A) expenses separately, for the entire business, and expressing it as a fraction of the COGS.

For example, if we were a large business with a COGS of $1B a year and spent another $100M a year on managerial salaries, travel that isn't tied directly to a program, R&D, B&P, etc., then we would conclude that our G&A rate is 10% of the COGS. We would have to add G&A on top of COGS to get to what is known as the Break-Even cost, sometimes called the Fully Accounted Break-Even (FABE) cost.

As we'll see in the chapter *The Rules of the Road* if you choose to do business with a Government they may have Cost Accounting Standards they will expect you to meet, which can complicate things a bit. But at this point, we've developed an appreciation for what it costs to build a product, or offer a service, and we've also seen how it's important to have a healthy margin – the difference between what it costs you to make the product and what you can sell it for. The amount you can sell it for is simply known as the price, so we need to examine pricing strategies.

PRICING

As we have seen, a key relation in accounting is

>Profit = Price – Cost

The business gets to calculate its costs, but the customer gets to determine the price. Quite simply, customers vote with their feet. They leave and go buy it from somewhere else if they think they can get a better value elsewhere.

> *How would a company know what price it should charge for its products or services?*

The answer is very dependent on the industry. In commercial businesses, such as the fast food industry, you sometimes hear the term "whatever the market will bear". That is, those business set prices based on what their customers are willing to pay.

Price too low and you will have a lot of customers, but you won't make a lot of profit on each unit. Go to the other extreme, price the unit too high, and you might not have many customers, but you would make a lot of profit on each unit. How would you know which strategy is best? Consider the following example.

If it takes you $1 to make a cup of coffee, you could choose to price it at $2, $3, or $4. At those prices you'd make a profit of $1, $2, or $3, respectively. You'd have to sell 3x the coffee at $2 per cup to make the same profit you'd make by selling it at $4 a cup. But you'd only have to sell 1.5x the coffee at $3 per cup to make that same profit. How would you know what way would maximize your profits? Often you learn by trial and error. Have a sale and see if that induces more people to buy your coffee. Raise prices a bit and see if anybody complains or stops buying it and react accordingly.

Of course, your cost accountant will tell you that whichever approach you take will have a ripple effect on your cost structure. If you sell 3x the coffee at $1 a cup, you now have to buy 3x more coffee, which may put you in a better position to negotiate lower unit prices since you're such a good customer for the coffee distributor. Sell the same coffee at $4 a cup, you don't sell as much, and your distributor may try to raise your prices since you're buying less.

One other important point to emphasize is the relation between price and profit. If you raise the price of your coffee from $2 per cup to $3 per cup that's a 50% price increase. But after you subtract the $1 it takes to cover your costs; your profit would go from $1 per cup to $2 per cup – a 100% increase. It's often the case that a small difference in price has a much greater impact on profits. That's why margins are so important. If you have a healthy margin you are better positioned to stay in business long term if you have to reduce your price to attract customers or fend off competitors.

In more high-tech industries, like aerospace and defense, pricing gets more complicated. How would you determine a sell price for a new airliner? Or for a new long-range bomber? When selling that airliner to a commercial airline, we're dealing with commercial pricing. What will the market bear?

But when selling a new long-range bomber to a Government, and we're thinking the Long Range Strike – Bomber (LRS-B) contract awarded in October 2015 by the United States Air Force, you would be offering your services to build a product that was customized to customer provided specifications. If you're trying to do business with your own Government, you typically must disclose your cost structure, and negotiate your profit. Often that process is like that shown in Table 10.

You would start by compiling a list of all your costs. You would probably have separate line items for labor, for material, for travel, and other types of expenses.

Table 10. Example Pricing Methodology.

Labor			
	Task A	$ 111,111	
	Task B	$ 222,222	
	...		
Material			
	Item A	$ 11,111	
	Item B	$ 22,222	
	...		
Travel			
	Trip A	$ 1,111	
	Trip B	$ 2,222	
	...		
	Subtotal Cost	**$ 369,999**	
	General & Admin	$ 111,000	30.0%
	Fully Accounted Break Even (FABE)	$ 480,999	
	Fee	$ 48,100	10.0%
	Cost of Money (COM)	$ 1,202	0.25%
	Price	**$ 530,301**	

What profit rates will be allowed by your Government?

(As we will see in Chapter 6, this should map to the Work Breakdown Structure (WBS) for the program.) The subtotal of all of those costs can be thought of as the internal price – the price we'd have to pay ourselves to do all the work. But it doesn't represent the full cost. First, we have to account for all of the General & Administrative (G&A) costs we discussed in the section on Financial Accounting. Those are typically a percentage of all of the other costs, and in this example, we've assumed they are 30%. Adding in G&A gets you to the Fully Accounted Break Even (FABE) cost of $480,999 as shown. This is the price you'd have to charge just to break even – it doesn't yet account for any profit. The next step would be adding on whatever profit you can charge, and in this example we've assumed 10%. (More on that in just a bit.)

Finally, we add on Cost of Money (COM). Cost of Money refers to the average interest rate at which you are able to borrow money. There is typically a delay between the time you submit an invoice for payment, and you receive the payment, and COM accounts for the interest you have to pay while you're carrying all of that cost. This isn't always added on – some customers would expect you to bear that cost yourself, but others will accept it's a reasonable cost of doing business and reimburse you for it. In this case, if we assume a 3.0% yearly interest rate, and a 30-day turnaround time for payment, the effective rate for COM is 3.0% / 12 = 0.25%. Finally, we get to a sell price of $530,301. At that sell price, you would generate a profit of $48,100.

In the US, profit calculations must consider the unique circumstances of the immediate negotiation. If you're selling the same "commercial" product to the Government that you'd sell to another company, then it may be deemed a "commercial" purchase, and special Government regulations may not apply. But if you're offering to build a unique product for the Government, expect them to look over your shoulder and make sure that your profit (also known as fee) is "reasonable". Who gets to determine "reasonable"? The Government of course.

In the US, the contract fee cannot exceed certain limits specified in the US Code (Law) or Code of Federal Regulations. For example, experimental, developmental, or research work performed under a Cost Plus Fixed Fee (CPFF) contract, (more on what exactly that means in a bit), is a maximum of 15%. For all other CPFF contracts, the maximum is 10% fee.

The US Federal Acquisition Regulation (FAR), (specifically FAR 15.404-4(d)), lists the factors that the US Government official, (e.g., the contracting officer), must consider when determining what fee is reasonable. This includes complexity; risk; independent investments; and so on. The greater the complexity, the risk to successful execution, or the amount of company money you invested in developing the capability to make a credible offer, the greater fee you may be able to negotiate.

Of course, when dealing with Government's, cost realism also comes into play. You can't lay an unrealistically low estimate on the table in hopes of winning the contract, and then overrun the original estimate significantly and expect the Government to bail you out. The Government will first do an independent assessment of what a realistic cost would be, using the technical and managerial approach you've outlined in your proposal. If they think your costs are unrealistically low, they will mark them up accordingly. In short, they will do a price analysis to confirm that the price you have proposed is both fair and reasonable. The Government isn't in the business of creating successful businesses by spending too much on its purchases, nor is it interested in getting such a good deal that it drives a company into bankruptcy. They simply want to be good stewards of the taxpayer's money.

Regardless of whether you're dealing with a commercial customer, or a Government customer, it all boils down to value. Does the customer feel that they are getting a good value for their money? If so, the door is open, and we can likely do business together. Of course, articulating the value that the customer is getting for its money is an art, and that is the subject of the next section.

VALUE PROPOSITION

The dictionary would define value as "the importance, worth, or usefulness of something". In business, it is vitally important that you understand who will buy your product (the market) and why they buy it (the value proposition).

In a free market, value is always determined by the buyer, not the seller. You can insist that I should be willing to buy a liter of water from you for $100. But if I only need walk around the corner to find one for sale for $1, I'd probably buy it from somebody else. As a customer, I get to determine the value.

A very important point to bear in mind is that small differences in value may result in huge differentials in pay. This is most obvious examples are found in professional sports. Look at the difference in pay between a National Basketball Association (NBA) first round draft pick, and a second-round draft pick, Table 11. The difference in pay is not a measure of the absolute difference in skill set, but of the relative difference.

Consider the statistics reported by Forbes for the highest paid athletes in the world in 2017, Table 12. As seen, the salary difference between the first ranked soccer player (Ronaldo) and the second ranked soccer player (Messi) is only 9% ($58M / $53M). If Ronaldo is 9% better at soccer than Messi, then why are his sponsorships 30% ($35M / $27M) larger? There is no simple answer to these questions, other than – it's what the market will bear. Ronaldo's sponsors "believe" that he is worth $35M per year.

A player, like Ronaldo or Messi, that doesn't get the offer they are hoping for from a particular soccer club, can change leagues, and still hope to find a better (more lucrative) offer. In some businesses, that's a reality of the market. In others, it's more like boxing – winner takes all.

Table 11. 2017 – 2018 NBA Rookie Salary.
(Source - //basketball.realgm.com/nba/info/rookie_scale)

Pick	1st Year Salary	2nd Year Salary	Total	Percent Increase Over Next Player
1	$5,855,200	$6,949,900	$12,805,100	11.8%
2	$5,238,800	$6,218,300	$11,457,100	11.4%
3	$4,704,500	$5,584,000	$10,288,500	10.9%
4	$4,241,700	$5,034,600	$9,276,300	10.4%
5	$3,841,000	$4,559,100	$8,400,100	10.1%
6	$3,488,600	$4,140,900	$7,629,500	9.5%
7	$3,184,700	$3,780,100	$6,964,800	9.2%
8	$2,917,600	$3,463,100	$6,380,700	8.8%
9	$2,681,900	$3,183,300	$5,865,200	5.3%
10	$2,547,700	$3,024,100	$5,571,800	5.3%
11	$2,420,400	$2,872,900	$5,293,300	5.3%
12	$2,299,400	$2,729,400	$5,028,800	5.3%
13	$2,184,400	$2,592,900	$4,777,300	5.3%
14	$2,075,300	$2,463,200	$4,538,500	5.3%
15	$1,971,300	$2,339,900	$4,311,200	5.3%
16	$1,872,900	$2,223,000	$4,095,900	5.3%
17	$1,779,200	$2,111,900	$3,891,100	5.3%
18	$1,690,300	$2,006,300	$3,696,600	4.7%
19	$1,614,100	$1,915,900	$3,530,000	4.2%
20	$1,549,500	$1,839,200	$3,388,700	4.2%
21	$1,487,500	$1,765,700	$3,253,200	4.2%
22	$1,428,100	$1,695,100	$3,123,200	4.2%
23	$1,371,000	$1,627,300	$2,998,300	4.2%
24	$1,316,200	$1,562,200	$2,878,400	4.2%
25	$1,263,500	$1,499,700	$2,763,200	3.4%
26	$1,221,600	$1,450,000	$2,671,600	3.0%
27	$1,186,300	$1,408,200	$2,594,500	0.6%
28	$1,179,100	$1,399,600	$2,578,700	0.7%
29	$1,170,500	$1,389,300	$2,559,800	0.7%
30	$1,162,100	$1,379,300	$2,541,400	NA

Table 12. The Highest Paid Athletes in the World.
(Source – www.forbes.com/athletes/)

Rank	Athlete	Sport	Salary ($M)	Sponsors ($M)
1	Cristiano Ronaldo	Soccer	$ 58	$ 35
2	LeBron James	Basketball	$ 31	$ 55
3	Lionel Messi	Soccer	$ 53	$ 27
4	Roger Federer	Tennis	$ 6	$ 58
5	Kevin Durant	Basketball	$ 27	$ 34
6	Andrew Luck	Football	$ 47	$ 3
7	Rory McIlroy	Golf	$ 16	$ 34
8	Stephen Curry	Basketball	$ 12	$ 35
9	James harden	Basketball	$ 27	$ 20
10	Lewis Hamilton	Auto Racing	$ 38	$ 8

There is only one heavyweight champion of the world, (though the International Boxing Federation, World Boxing Association, World Boxing Council, and World Boxing Organization all reserve the right to award that title independently). If you manage to win the "undisputed" title, you are number one in the world and there's no debate.

Consider the $55B (billion) contract award for the US Long Range Strike – Bomber (LRS-B). In October 2015 the US Air Force selected Northrop-Grumman. The second-place finisher, a team of Lockheed-Martin and Boeing, will get nothing. This example illustrates another important facet of the market –

you only need to be slightly better than the competition to gain a much larger market share.

Understanding the value proposition of your product in the eyes of your customer is critical. (The only thing more important is understanding your value proposition as an employee in the eyes of your employer.) Successful businesses combine knowledge of what the market wants, and the value proposition their product can deliver, into a Business model. This is the subject of the next section.

BUSINESS MODEL

A business model describes how an organization creates and delivers value. Examples of two different business models are shown in Table 13. Although the models are almost the exact opposite of one another in many ways, they both work because there is a large market – a large number of consumers – that want to take advantage of their respective value propositions. For Option A, the market is consumers that have sufficient spending cash to make it to the next pay check, but still want to minimize their yearly spending. For Option B, the market is consumers that don't have sufficient spending cash for lots of bulk purchases and need to focus on buying just enough to make it to the next pay check.

Consider the business model for most ink jet printers. On a recent trip to an office supply store, we found an ink jet printer – which contained two different ink jet cartridges (one black and one color) – retailing for $59.99. The black ink jet cartridge was being sold separately for $18.99 and the color cartridge for $22.99. Purchasing both cartridges would cost $41.98. It would therefore imply that the cost of the printer without cartridges was a mere $18.01.

Table 13. Simple Example of Different Business Models.

	Option A	Option B
Strategy	Offer low prices on high quantities of products	Offer low quantity options on the basic necessities
Result	Lower unit prices, but higher total price	Higher unit prices, but lower total prices
Market	Consumers with larger amounts of cash on hand who want to minimize their yearly expense	Consumers with small amounts of cash on hand who just want to make it to their next pay day

We suggest that the cost of the system of printer + cartridges is dominated by the cost of the printer itself. But that is not reflected in the price. The business model in this case seems to be one where the manufacturer is content to break even on the cost of the printer, knowing that once you have the printer in your office you will have no choice but to continue to buy their printer cartridges for the life of the machine. The profit margin on the ink cartridge is quite high and would guarantee the manufacturer a long-term stream of income at higher profit rates, when compared to the higher cost, but lower margin, sale of the printer itself.

Over the past generation, the business model of most car dealerships has evolved. Back in the day, you went to a car dealership for one thing – to purchase a car. The dealer, usually, made enough profit on each individual sale, and sold enough cars, to make a good living. But once the buyer left the dealership they wouldn't come back for several years, until they needed a new car. In between, the buyer – now owner and operator – needed to have regular preventive maintenance such as oil changes and tire rotations, and they also needed to get the vehicle repaired when it broke. For those lower cost, but more frequent, sales the car owner went to a mechanic. Today, most new car dealers also have a maintenance department and are going to great lengths to convince the car buyer that the dealership is the best value place for ongoing maintenance. They are moving from a business model based on a high value, but very infrequent sale, to one that also includes a large number of smaller sales on an ongoing basis.

If you're an engineer, you may be accustomed to splitting work into Non-Recurring Expense (NRE) and Recurring Expense (RE). As the name implies, NRE is the type of work that is done once and only once – such as the effort required to design a new piece of hardware or develop a new piece of software. RE is the type of work that occurs over and over – such as building the hardware. Your company's business model may treat NRE and RE very differently. If their core business is manufacturing, they may be content to make much lower profit on NRE, knowing that it will lead to more profitable RE in the long term. If the company is not a manufacturer but a designer, the business model may be built entirely around offering specialized NRE services that are not cost effective for companies to do in house since they do it very infrequently.

The purpose of this entire discussion is to highlight the fact that you will be a better engineer if you understand your products business model and value proposition. If you truly understand the products value proposition you will be able to make design trades that increase value in the eyes of the customer. If you truly understand the products business model you will be able to make design trades that increase the value of the product to the company's shareholder.

FORECASTING

We need to discuss one other topic before we move on, and that is forecasting. Whether you are a Government organization, or a for profit business traded on one of the major stock exchanges, the people who are subsidizing your existence – the tax payers or investors, respectively – want to get a feeling for how much money you're going to have to spend, and how much you're going to make, in the future. Hence the need for a disciplined forecasting process.

If you're a Government organization, you need to submit a budget for approval, and get confirmation that you do have authority to spend at the level requested. We'll talk about the US Government's process more in *The Rules of the Road*, but for now let's focus on a commercial business – one like the multitude of companies traded on one of the many stock markets around the world.

Although some investors no doubt choose to invest in specific companies because they want to be in that particular market or want to support that particular enterprise. However, most "professional" investors do it for the simple reason that they believe investing in company X is a good financial decision. In other words, it's an investment that balances their desire for a return on investment, in either the short or long term, with the resulting risk. Make no mistake, there is always risk. A company may predict world class sales and returns to its shareholders, but if you start to investigate the details there's always some underlying assumptions about specific contracts they may win, or how many people will go out and buy what they sell. If those assumptions don't prove to be correct, the business case will fall apart.

Where would you find the details about those assumptions? Back in the now familiar Annual Report. For profit companies issue a public report that summarizes their sales for the past year and includes their forecast for how bright the future will, or will not, be. Each quarter, companies update their sales forecast for the investment community, either confirming they are on plan, ahead of, or behind plan. (The professional investors – the "Wall Street" brokers – are the ones who buy and sell most shares of stock, so they are the ones the most readily influence stock prices.) The company's annual report is a public forecast that is used to assure the investment community that the company has a good plan for capturing the sales that will give the investors the return they desire. Does the public forecast discuss, in gory detail, all the things that might go wrong and derail the plan? Of course not! One of the rules in business – and in life –is: don't give the other guys bullets that they could shoot you with. While you need to be realistic, companies typically paint an optimistic picture – a glass half full view – of what the future of the business is like. Of course, at the same time, the competing companies are painting an equally realistic view of what their future will look like. Just remember, when you buy a stock, you're buying it from a person who's selling it because they either: i) need the cash right now; or ii) think it will be worth less in the future. Similarly, when you sell a stock you're typically selling it to someone who thinks it will be worth more in the future. Only one of you will be right.

Does that mean that budgeting and planning are not worthwhile? On the contrary, we think they are very valuable activities, but not because the results are incredibly accurate. Instead, because the process of creating a budget, or a plan, requires some hard analysis of the facts, and some realistic decision making about what truly is likely in the future. That is the value of the budgeting and planning process. If done correctly, it does help management make the hard decisions they have to make to keep the business viable in the long term. After all, we all want to work for companies that never have layoffs, and can maintain a stable, and growing, work force. But the reality of the 21st century is that this is extremely difficult to do over the long term. At the very least we want to work for companies that are realistic, and proactively take steps to improve the business in the short term, to insure long term viability.

Two important documents that most businesses generate, for internal consumption, are the Strategic & Financial Plan (S&FP) and the Annual Operating Plan (AOP). As its name implies, the S&FP is the result of the analysis the company conducts to determine how it can best achieve its strategic, and financial, goals and objectives. In other words, the S&FP describes what strategic investment of resources, (land, labor, and capital), the company must make– and how – to enable it to reach its financial objectives. Typically, this begins with an assessment of the overall business environment. Is the addressed market growing, shrinking, or staying stagnant? The company then asks, what would we realistically have to do to achieve our financial objectives? If last year's objective was 10% growth every year for the next five years, but this year the addressed market is expected to shrink by 10% due to factors beyond your control, the company has two options. 1.) Readjust their projections to something more realistic and achievable in the current market conditions; or 2.) Go "all in" and bet heavily on a plan that can take market share from the competition. Both strategies are viable, but – depending on the specifics – one may be more realistic than the other. The latter plan may require much more investment in land, labor, and capital, to win the orders that would fuel future growth. If that investment is just not affordable, then the company may have to readjust its expectations for short term growth to be more in line with what is affordable.

All of us are used to dealing with this on an individual basis every year. I may have planned on finally buying that new Sports Car next year, because after all I deserve it, but when the Orthodontist tells me that both of my kids will need an expensive set of braces, I may decide to buy a more affordable used mini-van instead.

As we said, the S&FP is typically an internal company document, and not released publicly. The reason for this is that the document would often contain information that could help the competition if they were to know about it. The S&FP may identify "must win" pursuits that the company is planning to invest heavily to win or may even acknowledge that they don't believe a particular market is going to be viable in the long term, so they're looking to exit that business. If the competition learned of those plans, they could take steps to block your strategy. To prevent that from happening, the S&FP is not released publicly.

Some notable exceptions to this are the strategic plans released by most government agencies. Many agencies are directed to create a strategy for future investments that use public funding. Those strategic plans are developed in public, and kept in the public eye, as a means of gathering support for the strategy. In the US, the National Science and Technology Council (NSTC) is responsible for coordinating Federal research and development. The Council coordinates research and development strategies across other Federal agencies to develop focused investment packages that can help achieve national goals. Those strategies are all summarized in publicly available documents, and other Government agencies are expected to show they follow the high-level strategy.

The S&FP is often a high-level plan that may cover five or more years into the future. We need a lot more detail for things that are closer at hand, and that's the purpose of the Annual Operating Plan (AOP). At its core, the AOP is the breakdown of what the company –or Government organization – thinks it can win (or spend) next year. Once the AOP gets finalized it's a commitment to the shareholders. It's the Chief Executive Officer's (CEOs) way of saying – we intend to win $10B in orders next year, I promise! To meet the AOP, it must flow down to each level in the organization. If the CEO has ten direct reports, then the CEO may simply assign each direct report the responsibility for winning $1B each. Now in reality, most business units aren't going to have the same potential for orders or sales, so some direct reports may be asked to bring in $1.2B because others can only realistically be expected to bring in $0.8B, and so on. Each of those direct reports, let's call them business unit leaders (typically Presidents or Vice-Presidents or General Managers), would look at their orders goal and then task their direct reports, let's call them Directors, with individual goals that – if met – would ensure the business unit would meet their goal.

The key to bear in mind is that it's not a one-way street. The CEO doesn't make up an order goal out of thin air and hand them out the various business units. Instead it's a negotiation. Each business unit is asked, what do you think you can realistically achieve? Those individually answers are rolled up at the company level and the CEO, and board of directors, ask – is that enough to keep the shareholders happy? Sometimes the answer might be yes, but often the shareholders will ask for a bit more, so the negotiations start.

"Can business unit X give me 10% more?"

"Well, there is a major pursuit we've been tracking, but we don't have enough B&P funds in our discretionary spending plan to submit a proposal and meet our other commitments. But if you give us more B&P money, we'll be able to submit a proposal and we think we would have a good chance of winning? So, if you give me more B&P, I'll sign up for more orders. Is it a deal?"

After all the internal negotiations cease, the result is the final AOP for the corporation that flows down to all the levels of the organization. If done properly, each business unit knows what it is expected to achieve in terms of orders, and sales, and also has a pretty good idea of the individual pursuits that it needs to win to meet its goal. If you planned to bid on 5 awards and hoped to win 3, but you actually won 4, you may be able to help another part of the organization that bid on 6, planned on winning 4, but only won 2.

As we've just discussed, there are many different layers of the organization, from the CEO and other C-Suite executives, to VPs, Directors, Managers, and so on. As a new engineer, it's important to appreciate what the different layers of the organization are focused on, so you can tailor your communications with them to provide the information they need to be successful. This is the point of the next chapter, *Navigating the Corporation*.

CHAPTER 3
NAVIGATING THE CORPORATION

In my company the engineers have a standing joke. They like to say that we have only two types of employees – engineers, and those who wish they were. While the engineers might chuckle at this, the rest of the organization probably won't. Still, I think it's an accurate stereotype of how engineers view the organization. If you're an engineer, you appreciate the distinction between hardware, firmware, and software engineering – the difference between computer, electrical and mechanical engineering – and so on. If you're an engineer – everybody else in the company falls into that big bucket known as "non-engineers". We hear somebody talk about financial accounting and cost accounting as though they are completely different things, and we think – but they were all business majors in college. Aren't all those business degrees fairly interchangeable?

At the same time, the accountants are no doubt doing the same thing to engineers. They might not appreciate the difference between hardware, firmware and software, but they know the difference between cost and financial accounting, and between contracts and subcontracts. We think it's important to understand the different parts of the organization. They are there for a reason after all, and this chapter will explore those differences.

In the previous chapter we mentioned several Aerospace and Defense corporations. If we look at job titles on their executive committees, Figure 4 and 5, we see a lot of non-engineering descriptions. Even when we look at organizational structures in the Government, such as the US National Aeronautics and Space Administration (NASA), Figure 6, or the Federal Aviation Administration (FAA), Figure 7, we see similar titles.

Figure 4. Boeing Executive Committee.

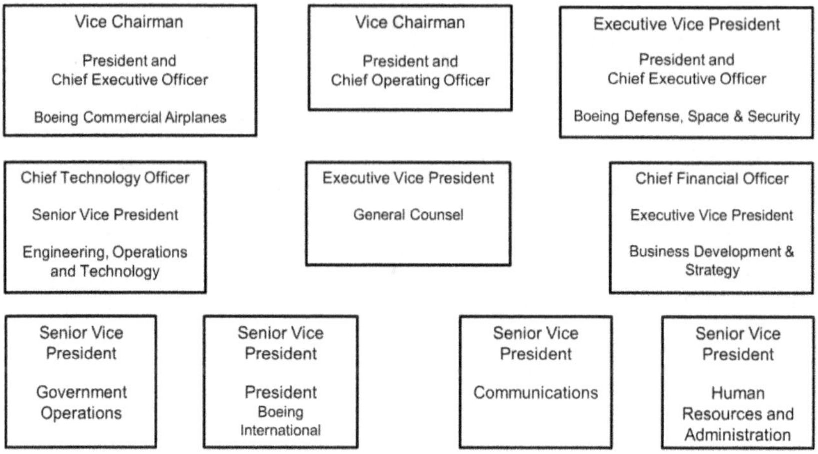

- Vice Chairman — President and Chief Executive Officer, Boeing Commercial Airplanes
- Vice Chairman — President and Chief Operating Officer
- Executive Vice President — President and Chief Executive Officer, Boeing Defense, Space & Security
- Chief Technology Officer — Senior Vice President, Engineering, Operations and Technology
- Executive Vice President — General Counsel
- Chief Financial Officer — Executive Vice President, Business Development & Strategy
- Senior Vice President — Government Operations
- Senior Vice President — President Boeing International
- Senior Vice President — Communications
- Senior Vice President — Human Resources and Administration

Figure 5. Airbus Group Executive Committee.

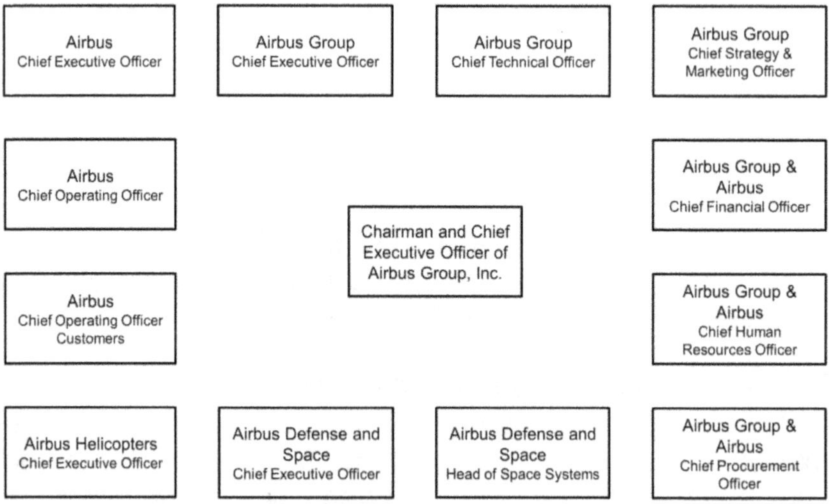

- Airbus Chief Executive Officer
- Airbus Group Chief Executive Officer
- Airbus Group Chief Technical Officer
- Airbus Group Chief Strategy & Marketing Officer
- Airbus Chief Operating Officer
- Airbus Group & Airbus Chief Financial Officer
- Chairman and Chief Executive Officer of Airbus Group, Inc.
- Airbus Chief Operating Officer Customers
- Airbus Group & Airbus Chief Human Resources Officer
- Airbus Helicopters Chief Executive Officer
- Airbus Defense and Space Chief Executive Officer
- Airbus Defense and Space Head of Space Systems
- Airbus Group & Airbus Chief Procurement Officer

54 • Tribble

Figure 6. NASA Organizational Structure.

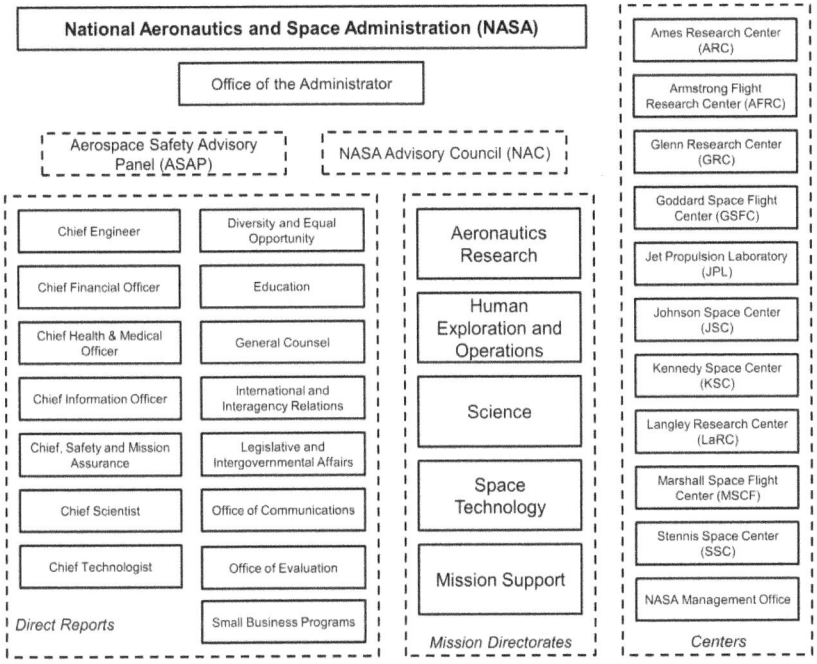

Figure 7. FAA Organizational Structure.

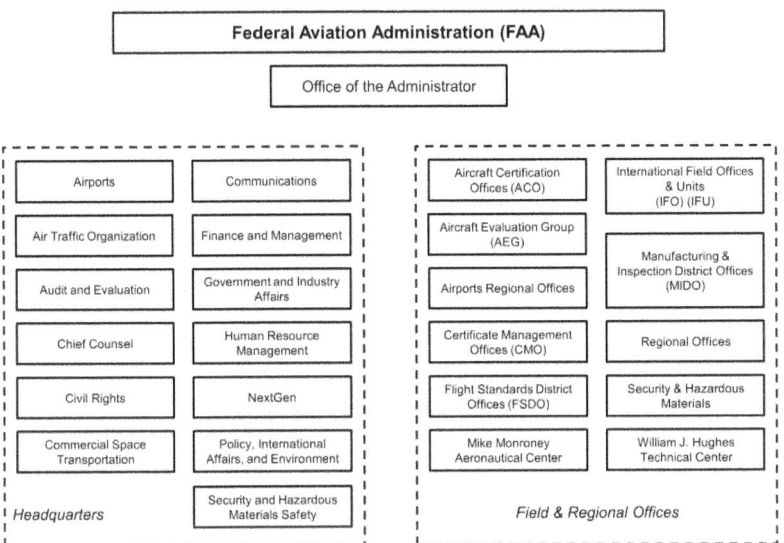

The previous four organizational charts had titles like

- Chief Engineer
- Chief Executive Officer (CEO)
- Chief Financial Officer (CFO)
- Chief Health & Medical Officer (CH&MO)
- Chief Human Resources Officer (CHRO)
- Chief Information Officer (CIO)
- Chief Operating Officer (COO)
- Chief Procurement Officer (CPO)
- Chief Safety & Mission Assurance Officer (CS&MAO)
- Chief Scientist
- Chief Strategy & Marketing Officer (CS&MO)
- Chief Technology Officer (CTO)

These positions, and others like them, form the "C-Suite" positions – the positions that start with "Chief", or head, and then clarify exactly what their responsibilities are. In general, the Chief Executive Officer (CEO) is the ultimate head of the corporation, reporting only to the Board of Directors, and the other C-Suite positions report to the CEO.

Of course, there are many other organizations, such as

- Communications
- General Counsel
- Government Operations

and if we drill down we'll find other titles like

- Business Development
- Engineering
- Manufacturing
- Program Management

and so on. The other parts of the organization are there for a reason, and you need to know when to involve them. A notional listing of the different parts of the organization you might find in a large high technology company is shown in Figure 8. Let's examine each of these individually.

Figure 8. Example Functional Areas.

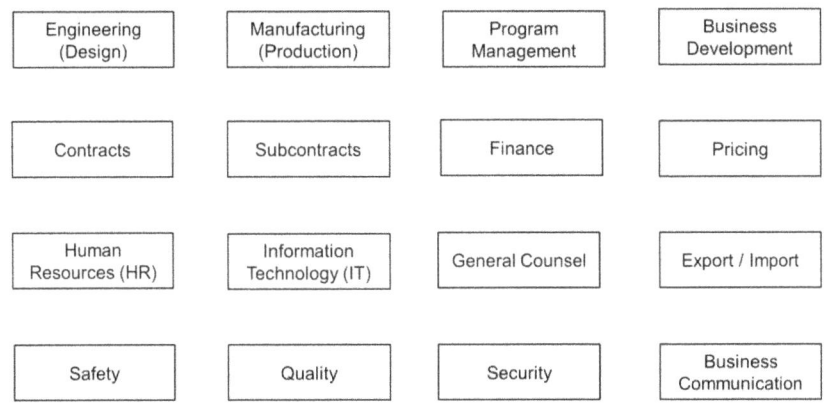

ORGANIZATIONAL STRUCTURE

Engineering

The part of the organization most responsible for the design and development of new products and services.

Often split by functional area such as Electrical Engineering or Mechanical Engineering, or by product line such as Aircraft or Spacecraft. Most engineers wind up here.

Manufacturing

Also known as production, or operations, the part of the organization most responsible for building and testing products.

Some engineers wind up here, but most of the people in the manufacturing organization are the technicians who build and test the products. (In the US, the distinction is that "engineers" typically have a four-year college degree, and focus on design, while "technicians" have a two-year degree, and focus on assembly or test. Of course, as products become more complex the trend is for engineers to become more involved in assembly and test.)

Note that engineering and manufacturing will likely have their own management chain, where you will find people with job titles like "engineering manager" or "manufacturing manager". The distinction is that those managers are responsible for staffing their respective organizations – for ensuring that they have enough qualified personnel to do the jobs that are expected to come their way. They are tasked to do the hiring when times are good, and do the layoffs when times are bad.

Program Management

The part of the organization ultimately responsible for profit and loss, and program execution.

Many engineers migrate from the technical ranks to the business leadership ranks and wind up in program management. A solid technical understanding of the challenges the design, or manufacturing, team is facing helps build your credibility. At the same time, your focus here is on managing the program and not solving all the problems for the new engineers.

The chapter on *Planning for Success* is devoted to explaining in more detail exactly what the program manager does and how they do it. The PM indirectly has a lot of feedback into a young engineer's career path. If they recognize you as a competent engineer and hard worker, they'll begin to ask for you by name for their next project, and that builds credibility in the eyes of your fellow engineers. At the same time, show the PM you can't be trusted to bring the tasks in on time and on budget, and they'll start asking for you to be assigned to other teams.

That kind of negative feedback will hinder your career. Outside of your own chain of command, program management has the most input on your job performance.

Business Development

The part of the organization responsible for developing new business opportunities.

Often composed of a sales group, which is responsible for selling products to customers; a marketing group, which is responsible for understanding what new product features the market is going to expect in the near future; and a strategy group, which is responsible for understanding how the company's business model may need to evolve to stay profitable in the future. Again, a lot of engineers migrate here. A sales person's job is to explain the technical features of your product to a prospective customer and help articulate its value proposition. It's a lot easier for them to do that if they have a technical background and understand the problem the customer is trying to solve.

Note that it's not unusual in the aerospace and defense industry to see a lot of former military officer's wind up in leadership roles, often in business development, where they wind up selling or marketing to the organization that they were formerly part of. From one perspective, that sounds great – who better to understand how the Air Force works than somebody who was in the Air Force for 30 years and just retired? At the same time, that creates the potential for a conflict of interest. If an Air Force Officer decides they're ready to retire, and starts looking for a civilian job, would they be able to be impartial when evaluating products and services provided by the company they're interviewing with? To avoid that potential conflict of interest most governments have regulations that require military personnel notify their chain of command before they start interviewing, so their commanding officer can confirm that they aren't working on anything that could even give the appearance of a conflict of interest. Similarly, companies are typically prohibited from even interviewing active duty military personnel until they can confirm that the proper paperwork is in place. How would you even know that's a requirement if you're an engineer? You wouldn't, unless somebody has explained that to you. That responsibility falls to the part of the organization known as Human Resources.

Human Resources (HR)

The part of the organization responsible for staffing the other parts of the organization, for ensuring that employee compensation and benefits are appropriate, and confirming that the company is complying with federal laws and regulations on hiring practices.

This includes programs like affirmative action in the US, positive discrimination in the UK, reservation in India, and employment equity in Canada.

HR is the part of the organization you turn to when you want to hire somebody. Although you'll have to help write the technical aspects of the job description, HR is there to get it posted to the company's web site, advertising it at job fairs, etc. They are also the ones who are charged with knowing what a fair and reasonable salary is for everybody else. Don't expect to get paid $250k a year, if there are a glut of qualified engineers looking for work who'd be glad to start at a mere $75k a year.

Of course, the other side of hiring is firing. If you're a manager, and you're having trouble with an employee, you turn to HR for help. They can advise you on how to deal with the issues appropriately, so that the problem employee honestly has an opportunity to address whatever the concerns are.

Note that there is a big difference between being laid off and being fired. Being laid off just means we ran out of money and couldn't afford to pay you anymore. Being fired means you weren't getting the job done. It's a performance issue. Firing someone is obviously difficult for the person being fired, but it's also difficult for the person doing the firing. If it has to happen, HR can explain the process to be followed and also remind the manager of the not so obvious steps that have to take place in those, hopefully, rare instances. For example, you probably want to collect the employee's computer, company credit card, and badge, and you will want to deactivate their computer passwords, so they can't decide to be vindictive and delete data from their computer later. The people who do that last step are of course the Information Technology (IT) group.

Information Technology (IT)

The part of the organization responsible for installing, maintaining, and securing the company's computing infrastructure.

These are the people you call when you've forgotten your password after that three-week cruise in the Bahama's, or when you power up your computer one morning and it freezes up. This is the organization that maintains the computing and network infrastructure, ensures that there is virus protection software in place, and that there is a firewall capable of preventing corporate espionage. Like the HR group, you might not think you have much of a need for a separate IT organization, until your computer freezes up and then they become indispensable. It's that way with most parts of the organization.

Contracts

The part of the organization responsible for receiving contracts from the customer and ensuring compliance with all the necessary terms and conditions.

This group is the one most responsible for understanding Government laws and regulations, like the US Federal Acquisition Regulation System.

Early in my career as an engineer, I never truly understood what those people in contracts did. They were the ones who got the formal notification that we were selected for the new program, or got additional funding for a project, and one day they just announced – okay, the paperwork's ready, you can begin working. I never really appreciated what was going on behind the scenes.

Now that I'm a program manager, I realize that the contracts manager is my best friend. The chief engineer may help find a solution to a difficult and challenging engineering problem, but the contracts manager will help keep me out of jail. It's their job to understand what we are required to do by the contract, and what we don't have to do at all.

On one of the programs I was supporting the end user wanted our software to work on two different computing platforms. Unfortunately, when they wrote the contract the statement of work clearly said that the software had to run on platform A OR B, not A AND B. As such, as much as the customer wanted it, we were not contractually obligated to do it. That's why it's important to know what the contract requires. If it's in the contract you have to do it. If it's not in the contract, you don't have to do it, and probably won't get paid for it if you do it anyway.

I also remember the day one of the engineers came to me and asked me how to charge the expenses for the trip he just took to give a presentation to the customer. I pointed out that our contract did not authorize us to bill our customer for travel expenses, and asked who authorized him to book travel and get on the plane in the first place? Being an engineer, and a good one at that, he said simply "Well, the customer asked me to come give a presentation. When they ask me to do something they have to pay for it, don't they?"

The answer to that question depends on who asked you to do it, and how. If the customers subcontracts manager asked you to do it and made it official by putting it in a letter to your contracts manager, then as soon as you sign the amendment to the contract it becomes binding. But if a junior engineer on the customer side asks you "can you come out here and explain it to my boss", then it's not official. Strictly speaking, they shouldn't ask you to do things that are "out of scope", but at the same time, you should know that you're supposed to say "no, I can't do that because it's out of scope" when that is the correct answer. Contracts is the organization that helps you understand those little details.

By the way, to tie this back to the concept of value proposition, if you make a habit of doing things that aren't required by the contract just because they're neat things to do, then you probably aren't adding much value to the program.

Subcontracts

Closely related to contracts is subcontracts. This is the part of the organization responsible for giving subcontracts to your suppliers and ensuring compliance with all the necessary terms and conditions.

That's the key difference – contracts receives, while subcontracts gives. It may seem subtle to us engineers, but if we insist that hardware engineering and software engineering aren't the same thing, we have to accept that there's a difference between contracts and subcontracts. When you need to buy something from a supplier, you talk to your subcontracts manager.

Finance

The part of the organization responsible for understanding and controlling the financial performance of the organization.

This may include groups like pricing, program planning and control, financial and cost accounting, etc.

The finance organization is often led by the Chief Financial Officer (CFO), one of the key C-Suite executives, who is responsible for managing the financial risks of the corporation, preparing financial reports for shareholders, etc. Within the finance organization you often find a job description like controller, or comptroller. I remember early in my career I literally bumped into one of the executives in the hallway, and after making my apologies, I introduced myself and asked, "What do you do?" She replied, "I'm the controller", and then went merrily on her way as I stood there asking myself "I wonder what she controls?"

Today, I know that the controller is there to control cash flow. Their job is to make sure we have enough cash in the bank to pay our bills. How do they do that? Probably the same way you balance your own personal checking account, by making sure that you get your paycheck from your employer before you start paying your bills. In the case of a large corporation, you simply make sure that your customers are paying you before you start paying your suppliers, and employees. It may sound easy, but it's not, and it's very important. If you don't have enough money on hand to pay your employees, you have big problems. People rarely offer to work for free, and if you can't even make payroll your shareholders will start to wonder how you're going to manage to stay in business, let alone grow and give them the return on their investment that they're looking for.

Down in the depths of the finance organization you will find people who specialize in tracking costs – how much did your project spend last month, and how much longer can you continue that trend before you go over budget; or in calculating prices – what do we need to charge for our new widget to cover all of our costs and make a profit. A lot of that task requires a thorough understanding of exactly where the organization accrues costs, and how you can pay for those in accordance with standard accounting practices.

There are a lot more parts of the organization that we haven't begun to touch on yet. We'll mention a few others briefly.

Export / Import

The part of the organization responsible for understanding how to legally export products from, or import products into, the country of origin.

In the United States the export compliance group is responsible for understanding the details of the Export Administration Regulations (EAR) and the International Traffic in Arms Regulations (ITAR). Similarly, the import compliance group is responsible for understanding the details of import regulations.

Again, until you investigate the details you really don't appreciate the complexities that can arise here. On one program we were delivering a piece of hardware to a customer in Sweden. The customer wanted to make sure that the holes on our piece of hardware lined up with the holes on their hardware, so they shipped us one of their mounts.[2] The mount was basically two flat pieces of metal, parallel to each other, with some rubber shock absorbers in between. The holes on the top metal plate lined up with the holes our hardware, and the holes on the bottom metal plane lined up with other holes on a Swedish military vehicle. Now because the final user was indeed the Swedish military, when the mount showed up in the US customs office we got a call asking where our permit for importing Swedish military hardware was. I tried pointing out that it was two pieces of metal with rubber shock absorbers, so what was the big deal, but the customs office was unsympathetic. If its

---

[2] Yes, we know you can check this digitally, and we did. But the customer wanted to be very sure so we checked it manually as well.

"military" hardware you need an import license. In the chapter on *Globalization* we'll look at the import and export requirements in more detail.

Quality Assurance

The part of the organization responsible for ensuring that the proper quality control measures are in place and working properly.

Often this group is deliberately kept separate from engineering or manufacturing just to ensure that they bring an unbiased view to the task at hand. If you let the engineer run the acceptance test for a project she designed and built, she just might be motivated to try and find a way to make it pass the test even if the performance was marginal. Just to avoid the appearance of a possible conflict, quality is often separated out.

Safety

The part of the organization responsible for ensuring the safety of the workplace, and the products delivered.

As with quality, the safety organization is often a separate department to ensure that they keep the best interests of the organization, its customers, and its employees in mind.

Security

The part of the organization responsible for ensuring the physical security of the workplace.

This is the group responsible for making sure that nobody gets into the building without a badge, for getting temporary badges for people who forget theirs, for helping medical personnel navigate their way through the building if an employee is having a medical emergency, and so on.

Note that on government programs that require a security

clearance, there will probably be a part of the security organization assigned to managing that process. That is, they will be responsible for ensuring that only personnel with the right clearance are given access to classified information, and that the proper physical safeguards are in place for securing classified information.

General Counsel

Often called the Office of the General Counsel (OGC), this is the part of the organization responsible for ensuring legal compliance with all appropriate laws and regulations.

This could take on a number of different forms, such as employment law or contract law. There could also be a part of the Office of General Counsel responsible for managing the company's portfolio of Intellectual Property (IP). Are there designs that we're especially proud of that we want to make sure we have exclusive rights to, so we should patent them? If we do that, we can use that design for a specified period of time, but after the patent expires others can also use it. If I'm so proud of the design that I think I may never want to let others use it, then I can call it a trade secret and never tell anybody else about it. The recipe for Coca Cola™ is a trade secret, not a patent. If it were a patent, the patent would eventually expire and everybody else could use the same recipe. Of course, if anybody else ever figures out how to duplicate their trade secret the Coca Cola™ company won't be able to prevent them from selling a competing product, but the risk of that happening is outweighed by the opportunity to continue to sell Coca Cola™ in perpetuity.

Communications

The part of the organization responsible for issuing formal communications with the outside world.

This may include press releases of new products, new services, or significant contract wins. Sorry, but as a new engineer your opinion may not accurately reflect corporate policy.

ORGANIZATIONAL HIERARCHY

We just spent several pages talking about the different parts of the organization. Within each organization there is often also a clear organizational hierarchy. Rank and file engineers may report to a manager, who in turn reports to a director, who reports to a vice president, and so on as shown in Figure 9. Ultimately, the chain of command typically ends with one of the C-Suite positions – any of the Chief (fill in the blank) Officers, that ultimately report to the Chief Executive Officer (CEO). The CEO in turn reports to the Corporate Board of Directors. Terminology varies by company, and culture. For example, the term General Manager (GM) is used more often in the United States, while the term Managing Director (MD) is used more often in Europe or Asia.

Figure 9. Example Hierarchy.

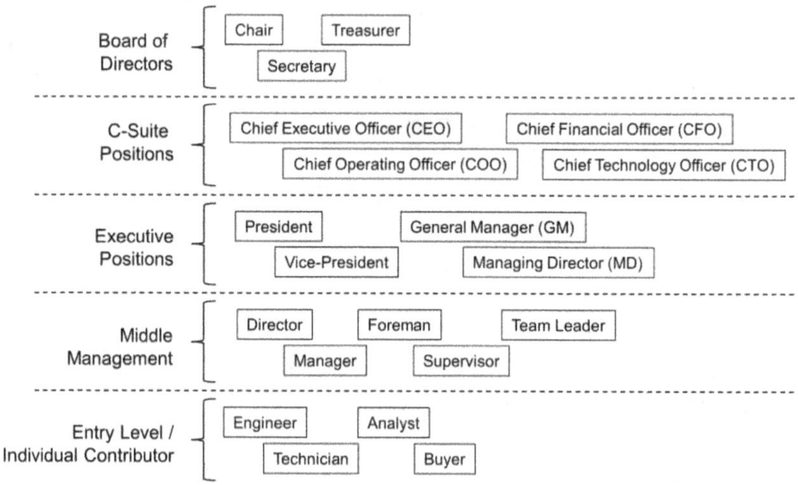

Level	Positions
Board of Directors	Chair, Treasurer, Secretary
C-Suite Positions	Chief Executive Officer (CEO), Chief Financial Officer (CFO), Chief Operating Officer (COO), Chief Technology Officer (CTO)
Executive Positions	President, General Manager (GM), Vice-President, Managing Director (MD)
Middle Management	Director, Foreman, Team Leader, Manager, Supervisor
Entry Level / Individual Contributor	Engineer, Analyst, Technician, Buyer

What changes as you move up the organizational structure? Not only your responsibility, and pay, but also your area of concern. As shown in Table 14, at the lower levels of the organization you are very focused on personal performance, and engineers at this level are often focused on designing or building products that meet specific Technical Performance Measures (TPM).

Table 14. Concerns and Metrics Change as you Move up in the Organization.

Level	Concern	Metrics
Board of Directors / C-Suite	• Shareholder Value	• Stock price; • Dividends; ...
Executives	• Contribution to Earnings • Market Share • Margins	• Balance Sheet; • Statement of Financial Position; ...
Mid-Level	• Cost • Schedule	• Earned Value Management (EVM)
Entry Level	• Technical	• Technical Performance Measures (TPM)

These TPMs are often defined in the product specification. Move up a level to mid-management and you start to focus more on cost and schedule. Are we getting the work done within our cost and schedule targets? As we will see in a later Section, Earned Value Management (EVM) is a technique used on many large programs to monitor cost and schedule.

Move up to the executive level and we start to worry about the business as a whole and not just the individual project or product line. How viable is our entire business? What market share do we have? What profit margins are we able to maintain, and so on? They monitor these metrics through tools such as the balance sheet or statement of financial position reflected in the company's annual report. (Other tools like the BCG Matrix and GE / McKinsey matrix are discussed in *Evaluating Success*).

Finally, at the highest level – the board of directors and C-Suite positions – we worry about the company as a whole. How is our stock price? Is it going up or going down? Why are investors picking another company over our company, and so on?

Appreciating the other metrics used to judge business success is very important when it comes to growing into more senior positions as an engineer or moving to other parts of the organization. Specifically, understanding how to adjust your message as you meet with people higher up the organizational structure is a unique, and valued, talent. Some of the best engineers we've known have the unique ability to spend a week in a conference room with a dozen Ph.D.'s working on very detailed technical analysis and can then walk into the CEOs office and explain what all of that technical analysis means to the business. If you want to be more valued as an engineer, or as a business leader, cultivate this ability.

Note that one question almost every organization struggles with is – how should we be organized?   Figure 10 shows the two basic options, which we will call vertical or horizontal.

In a vertically oriented hierarchy, the "engineering" column in the figure above, all the engineers may be in a single organization. They may report to a President or Vice-President of Engineering, who in turn reports to the CEO. This makes it nice and crisp in that every engineer works for the same overall organization.

Figure 10. Vertical and Horizontal Organizational Structures.

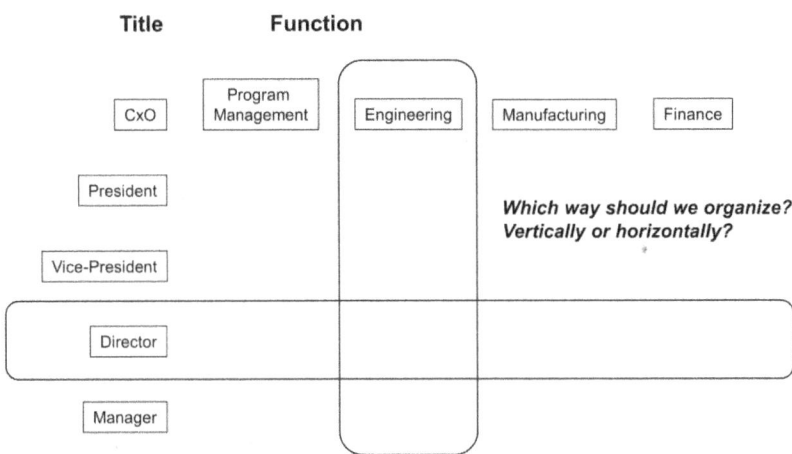

Within the Engineering organization there are no doubt different directors and managers that manage smaller and smaller groups of engineers, until you find the small groups of a dozen or so specialized engineers all working in the same group. In this hierarchy, the engineering managers would be responsible for coordinating with their counterparts in the other parts of the organization – typically program management or manufacturing – to ensure sure that all the engineers in their group had work to do. If there was more work to do than there were engineers available, we'd start thinking about hiring more engineers. If there were more engineers available than work to do, we'd start spreading the word that we had talented people who needed something to do – and ask if other parts of the organization needed help.

With the other organizational paradigm, which we will call horizontal, you might find that a Director had complete responsibility for an entire product line. They would have the program managers to worry about profit and loss, they would have engineers to design new products, manufacturing to build those products, as well as a finance group to monitor and control the costs.

Which organizational paradigm works best? In practice, there is no single right or wrong answer. It all depends on the organization in question, its products and services, its customers and so on. In our experience, over time organizations will flip flop from one to the other. Spend a few years in a vertical oriented structure, and you might conclude that the Directors, who have responsibility for profit and loss, might not have enough control over engineering and manufacturing, so you switch to a horizontal structure. After a few years in a horizontal structure, you might conclude that it's too hard to move engineers from one part of the organization to the other when the workloads were unbalanced, so you switch back to a vertical structure.

In the previous sections we've made several references to the Government, or Government organizations. In many high-tech industries, like aerospace and defense, the Government may be your best customer. There aren't many commercial companies that have a business case for purchasing attack helicopters. After all, it would be against the law for a commercial company to use them for their intended purpose, so what's the point?

If the Government is your customer, they probably have specific laws and regulations that mandate how they must conduct business, to ensure that the taxpayers (their shareholders) are getting a good value for the money. Even if you do business with other companies, the Government will probably have laws and regulations that you have to follow to ensure that you conduct business legally and aren't subject to any fines or penalties. The next chapter is devoted to understanding how Government's define *The Rules of the Road* that mandate how business must be conducted.

CHAPTER 4
THE RULES OF THE ROAD

It is obvious to the most casual observer that any business that wishes to remain in business must operate in accordance with the laws of the country it is based in. The specifics will vary from country to country, but in general each country's legal system will have a hierarchy that determines what portion of the law supersedes the other portions in the event of a conflict. For example, at the very foundation may be a Constitution, a body of fundamental principles that specify how the country is to be governed. Right behind the Constitution, would be Laws – a set of rules that everybody must follow or face penalties; and behind the Laws would be Regulations – additional rules, or directives that expand on the laws. The distinction between Laws and Regulations is often the Governing body that passed them. Laws are often passed by the Legislative branch of Government, while Regulations are often issued by the Executive branch of the Government, with the intention of clarifying more detailed points that weren't addressed in the Laws.

We'll look at a specific example in just a moment, but before we do let's ask a simple question

What is the purpose of these Government laws and regulations?

Let's be honest, reaching consensus on a simple answer to that simple question could be quite difficult, as most individuals would tend to color their answer based on their own political views. We'd probably never agree on exactly what the complete purpose is, but most of us would probably agree that a key purpose is

To protect individual rights

Think about it. Not everybody likes the referee, but you can't play the World Cup (or Super Bowl), without one. Given human nature, things can get out of hand if nobody enforces the rules.

Simply stated, good government protects individual rights with reasonable regulations. Citizens can spend less time defending their possessions, and more time doing other things like start a business. Bad governments either don't protect rights or put in place unreasonable regulations. Excessive regulation goes hand in hand with corruption. Government bureaucrats throw up hurdles so that they can extort bribes from those who seek to get over or around them.[3]

To see a specific example of how these Laws and Regulations affect business we'll take a quick look at the Laws and Regulations in the United States, the country that accounts for 25% of the gross world product. US business owners need to be aware of these when they conduct business. Laws and Regulations in other countries will no doubt be different, though some of the basic principles may be the same. If you need specifics, take your favorite attorney to lunch. (You'll find them in your company's Office of General Counsel as we saw in the last chapter.)

In the United States, legal hierarchy is the US Constitution first, followed by the laws passed by acts of Congress, treaties ratified by the Senate, regulations promulgated by the Executive branch, and case law originating from decisions made by the Judicial branch. (There is a similar hierarchy within each of the states for additional laws and regulations enacted at the state or local level.) The United States Code (USC) is the official listing of US laws, while the US Code of Federal Regulations (US CFR) is the official listing of US regulations.

---

[3] Wheelan, C., *Naked Economics: Undressing the Dismal Science,* W.W. Norton and Company.

EXAMPLE: US LAWS AND REGULATIONS

The laws of the United States (US) are contained in the US Code, which is prepared by the Office of the Law Revision Counsel of the United States House of Representatives. As shown in Table 15 the US Code is divided into 54 titles that represent broad subject areas.[4]

The regulations of the US are contained in the US Code of Federal Regulations (CFR), which is compiled by the Office of the Federal Register (OFR), an agency of the National Archives and Records Administration (NARA), and printed by the Government Printing Office (GPO). As shown in Table 16, the US CFR is divided into 50 titles that represent broad subject areas.[5]

As you can easily see from a side by side comparison, roughly half of the titles are identical between the Code and the CFR. We won't go into detail here, but a quick look at some of the topics is beneficial, just to appreciate the breadth and depth of the laws and regulations enacted. Specifically, we think it's important to understand:

- Taxation
    - Title 26 in both the Code and CFR;

- Intellectual Property
    - a combination of Title 17 – Copyrights and Title 35 – Patents, in the Code and Title 37 – Patents, Trademarks, and Copyrights in the CFR;

---

[4] If you want the gory details on the Code, an unofficial online version is available at: http://uscode.house.gov/

[5] If you want the gory details on the CFR, an unofficial online version is available at: www.ecfr.gov.

Table 15. The Contents of the US Code.

#	Name	#	Name
1	General Provisions	28	Judiciary and Judicial Procedure
2	The Congress	29	Labor
3	The President	30	Mineral Lands and Mining
4	Flag and Seal, Seat of Government, and the States	31	Money and Finance
5	Government Organization and Employees	32	National Guard
6	Domestic Security	33	Navigation and Navigable Waters
7	Agriculture	34	Navy (since repealed, and moved to Title 10)
8	Aliens and Nationality	35	Patents
9	Arbitration	36	Patriotic Societies and Observances
10	Armed Forces	37	Pay and Allowances of the Uniformed Services
11	Bankruptcy	38	Veterans Benefits
12	Banks and Banking	39	Postal Service
13	Census	40	Public Buildings, Properties, and Works
14	Coast Guard	41	Public Contracts
15	Commerce and Trade	42	The Public Health and Welfare
16	Conservation	43	Public Lands
17	Copyrights	44	Public Printing and Documents
18	Crimes and Criminal Procedure	45	Railroads
19	Customs Duties	46	Shipping
20	Education	47	Telecommunications
21	Food and Drugs	48	Territories and Insular Possessions
22	Foreign Relations and Intercourse	49	Transportation
23	Highways	50	War and National Defense
24	Hospitals and Asylums	51	National and Commercial Space Programs
25	Indians	52	Voting and Elections
26	Internal Revenue Service	53	*In Review*
27	Intoxicating Liquors	54	National Park Service and Related Programs

Table 16. The Contents of the US Code of Federal Regulations.

#	Name	#	Name
1	General Provisions	26	Internal Revenue
2	Grants and Agreements	27	Alcohol, Tobacco Products and Firearms
3	The President	28	Judicial Administration
4	Accounts	29	Labor
5	Administrative Personnel	30	Mineral Resources
6	Domestic Security	31	Money and Finance: Treasury
7	Agriculture	32	National Defense
8	Aliens and Nationality	33	Navigation and Navigable Waters
9	Animals and Animal Products	34	Education
10	Energy	35	Reserved (formerly Panama Canal)
11	Federal Elections	36	Parks, Forests, and Public Property
12	Banks and Banking	37	Patents, Trademarks, and Copyrights
13	Business Credit and Assistance	38	Pensions, Bonuses, and Veterans' Relief
14	Aeronautics and Space	39	Postal Service
15	Commerce and Foreign Trade	40	Protection of Environment
16	Commercial Practices	41	Public Contracts and Property Management
17	Commodity and Securities Exchanges	42	Public Health
18	Conservation of Power & Water Resources	43	Public Lands: Interior
19	Customs Duties	44	Emergency Management and Assistance
20	Employees' Benefits	45	Public Welfare
21	Food and Drugs	46	Shipping
22	Foreign Relations	47	Telecommunication
23	Highways	48	Federal Acquisition Regulations System
24	Housing and Urban Development	49	Transportation
25	Indians	50	Wildlife and Fisheries

- How the Government Buys Stuff
    - Title 48 – Federal Acquisition Regulation System in the CFR. We'll also bring in the Truth in Negotiations Act (TINA), which is buried in Title 10 – Armed Forces, in the Code.

We will discuss each of these topics briefly in the sections that follow. In the Appendix, we do deep dive on the laws and regulations that affect the aviation and space exploration industries, to show how a lot of the terminology that is used liberally in those industries has its origins in the US Code or CFR.

TAXATION

Revenue collection, based on taxes, is all part of the US Code and CFR Title 26 – Internal Revenue. In the Code, Subtitle A deals with Income Taxes; Subtitle B with Estate and Gift Taxes; and so on. Similarly, in the CFR, Subtitle A – Income Tax, you find Section 1.1-1 specifying the Income Tax on Individuals, and Section 1.11-1 specifying the Income Tax on Corporations. Other sections of Title 26 deal with tax credits, etc.

As most people appreciate, the tax rates on individuals (e.g., employees) are different than the tax rates on corporations. The amount of money that can be deducted or excluded is also different. We won't belabor the details of tax rates, but we will note that governments can create an incentive, or disincentive, through their tax policy. Allowing a corporation to deduct the expenses associated with internal research and development, or construction of new facilities, from their income statement creates an incentive for those activities for example. As we will re-examine in the chapter on Globalization, different countries have different corporate tax rates which can create an incentive to move work between countries.

Ensuring that you understand the tax rates on corporations become more challenging as your company expands and begins to deliver products, and hire employees, internationally. Larger corporations may have a Taxation group that specializes in understanding these details so that they can comply with the law and incorporate the latest tax implications in their analysis of future business opportunities.

INTELLECTUAL PROPERTY

We said that the purpose of government is to protect individual rights. In the Code, you see this addressed in both Title 17 – Copyrights and Title 35 – Patents. In the CFR this is combined into Title 37 – Patents, Trademarks, and Copyrights. In short, these Titles are where individuals, or corporations, have the right to protect their own inventions. Just to clarify the distinction in terminology

> A patent is a government authority or license conferring a right or title for a set period, especially the sole right to exclude others from making, using, or selling an invention.
>
> A trademark is a symbol, word, or words legally registered or established by use as representing a company or logo.
>
> A copyright is the exclusive legal right, given to an originator or an assignee to print, publish, perform, film, or record literary, artistic, or musical material, and to authorize others to do the same.

So, if you come up with a new invention that can add value to your customers, you have the right to patent that invention. You can also trademark a name for it. If you're an author, you can copyright written materials – like this book – to prevent others from taking your property – your inventions – and selling them to your customers, thereby depriving you of the opportunity.

The broader term used is Intellectual Property (IP). The World Intellectual Property Organization defines IP as follows:

> Intellectual Property refers to creations of the mind, such as inventions; literary and artistic works; designs; and symbols, names and images used in commerce.

As we saw in the previous chapter, most corporations have legal counsel that specialize in IP, (e.g., patents, trademarks, etc.), so they can proactively avoid infringing on existing patents, as well as secure other patents for new inventions. Some companies made a great deal of money by licensing their patents to others in exchange for a royalty fee.

One point to emphasize is that there are different types of patents. A design patent protects the design, of course, while a utility patent protects the function. That's an important distinction. One early example of the importance of a utility patent is the 1906 Wright Brothers US patent, #812393, for a "Flying Machine". Although the basic method used by the Wright Brothers for controlling the attitude of the aircraft was "wing warping", the fact that they had a patent for a "Flying Machine" enabled them to win patent infringement lawsuits against other early aviators, such as Glenn Curtiss, who used "ailerons" as a different method of control. (By the way, ailerons are now the standard method in the modern age.)

Another important point to emphasize is that there are differences in patent law between countries. Some of these differences may include:

- First to file versus first to invent
    - Were you the first to invent the new design or function, or simply the first to file the patent application? In most countries the first person to file gets the patent, even if the second person can prove that they had the idea first but failed to file a patent.

- Grace period
    - Grace period refers to the time you have between the time you make the information about your invention publicly available, and the time you file for the patent. In some countries you have a grace period, in other countries you don't.

    - Making the information publicly available includes giving a lecture about the invention, showing it to an investor without a Non-Disclosure Agreement (NDA), publishing it in a magazine, and so on. For that reason, most companies insist that an NDA is in place before they share anything that could be considered "proprietary information" with any third party. If it turns out that the information shared could have been the source of a patent, and the third party shared the information publicly, the person who originated the information has some legal recourse. (In other words, if you or your company signed a NDA, be sure you abide by the terms of it.)

The bottom line is you must file for patent protection separately in the countries where you expect to do business if you want that legal protection. How you file for that protection, and how long you have to file before you lose that right, varies by country. When in doubt, consult your favorite patent attorney.

One brief bit of foreshadowing before we move on, but you will also find IP addressed in the US Federal Acquisition Regulations, specifically Subpart 27. This Subpart clarifies the rights the US Government gets when it pays for something, as well as the rights the provider can maintain when delivering something to the US Government. A term encountered on many government procurements is Government Purpose Rights (GPR). GPR gives the government the right to use the information, or product, without restriction inside the government, while allowing the developer to continue to use the information, or product, outside of the government. So, if the government pays for it they can reuse it on other government programs, but they can't use it outside of the government and create competition. Confirming the IP rights that a contractor can maintain, and that the government gets, is an important part of many procurements.

FEDERAL ACQUISITION REGULATION SYSTEM

One important point that we need to discuss is how the US government – a significant customer in many industries – makes purchases. The regulations system that specifies how the US Government makes purchases is specified in Title 48 of the CFR – Federal Acquisition Regulations System   Chapter 1 of Title 48, the Federal Acquisition Regulation (FAR), is the principal set of rules in the Federal Acquisition Regulation System. The remaining Chapters of the FAR System consist mostly of supplements issued by various agencies of the federal government. For example, Chapter 2 is the Defense FAR Supplement, Chapter 3 is the Health and Human Services Supplement, and so on.

The FAR, Table 17 and 18, is the source of most of the regulations, and terminology, that we encounter in government procurements. A short review can help clarify where some of the practices and procedures originate.

Table 17. Chapter 1 – Federal Acquisition Regulation.

Subchap. Part	Title
A	**General**
1	Federal Acquisition Regulations System
2	Definitions of Words and Terms
3	Improper Business Practices and Personal Conflicts of Interest
4	Administrative Matters
B	**Acquisition Planning**
5	Publicizing Contract Actions
6	Competition Requirements
7	Acquisition Planning
8	Required Sources of Supplies and Services
9	Contractor Qualifications
10	Market Research
11	Describing Agency Needs
12	Acquisition of Commercial Items
C	**Contracting Methods and Contract Types**
13	Simplified Acquisition Procedures
14	Sealed Bidding
15	Contracting by Negotiation
16	Types of Contracts
17	Special Contracting Methods
18	Emergency Acquisitions
D	**Socioeconomic Programs**
19	Small business programs
20	Reserved
21	Reserved
22	Application of Labor Laws to Government Acquisitions
23	Environment, Energy and Water Efficiency, Renewable Energy Technologies, Occupational Safety, and Drug-Free Workplace
24	Protection of Privacy and Freedom of Information
25	Foreign Acquisition
26	Other Socioeconomic Programs

Table 18. Chapter 1 – Federal Acquisition Regulation, Continued.

Subchap. Part	Title
E	**General Contracting Requirements**
27	Patents, Data, and Copyrights
28	Bonds and Insurance
29	Taxes
30	Cost Accounting Standards Administration
31	Contract Cost Principles and Procedures
32	Contract Financing
33	Protests, Disputes, and Appeals
F	**Special Categories of Contracting**
34	Major System Acquisition
35	Research and Development Contracting
36	Construction and Architect-Engineer Contracts
37	Service Contracting
38	Federal Supply Schedule Contracting
39	Acquisition of Information Technology
40	Reserved
41	Acquisition of Utility Services
G	**Contract Management**
42	Contract Administration and Audit Services
43	Contract Modifications
44	Subcontracting Policies and Procedures
45	Government Property
46	Quality Assurance
47	Transportation
48	Value Engineering
49	Termination of Contracts
50	Extraordinary Contractual Actions and the Safety Act
51	Use of Government Sources by Contractors

Subchapter A, Part 3 – Business Practices

This subpart clarifies that it is against the law for government contracting officers to accept gifts or gratuities from contractors, and it is also against the law for contractors to give gifts to government employees. Obviously, gift giving / receiving could bias the outcome of a fair and open competition if the practice were allowed. Similarly, a company cannot write the specification for a new system and then submit a bid to build the system. Their intimate knowledge of the system could give them a competitive advantage. (This is known as an Organizational Conflict of Interest (OCI).) Companies that attempt to engage in these types of practices can be barred from federal contracts. Many US Government contractors require their employees to take explicit training on this point to avoid any confusion.

Subchapter C, Part 16 – Contract Types

You probably have a contracts management group within your organization that is responsible for understanding the FAR and ensuring your company is compliant when bidding on a US Government program. However, there are a couple of important points in the FAR that all engineers need to appreciate. The first, and most important, are the different types of contracts that can be used, Part 16 – Types of Contracts.

The FAR specifies several different types of contracts but the most important ones to be familiar with are: Firm Fixed Price (FFP), Cost Plus Fixed Fee (CPFF), Time & Material (T&M), and Indefinite Delivery Indefinite Quantity (IDIQ). We'll review each of these briefly.

Firm Fixed Price (FFP)

Quoting from the FAR

> A firm-fixed-price contract provides for a price that is not subject to any adjustment on the basis of the

contractor's cost experience in performing the contract. This contract type places upon the contractor maximum risk and full responsibility for all costs and resulting profit or loss. It provides maximum incentive for the contractor to control costs and perform effectively and imposes a minimum administrative burden upon the contracting parties. The contracting officer may use a firm-fixed-price contract in conjunction with an award-fee incentive (see 16.404) and performance or delivery incentives (see 16.402-2 and 16.402-3) when the award fee or incentive is based solely on factors other than cost. The contract type remains firm-fixed-price when used with these incentives.

The key take away is that a Fixed Price contract may be used when the risk is minimal. For example, when you're under contract to deliver additional quantities of the same product you've already delivered in the past. If you've delivered 100 radar systems for a fighter aircraft, and the government decides to install those same radar systems on 100 different aircraft, the government would likely push for a Firm Fixed Price (FFP) contract. With a FFP contract you would negotiate a sell price, to include a profit or fee for the contractor, and the contractor would then be responsible for delivering the radios at that fixed price. If the contractor has unexpected troubles and it costs more to deliver than they planned, then the contractor makes less profit at the end of the day. The government doesn't reimburse the contractor for the additional expense. At the same time, if the contractor finds unexpected efficiencies and it costs less to deliver than they planned, then contractor makes more profit at the end of the day. The government doesn't pay less because of the additional savings. FFP contracts minimize the financial risk to the government – the price is agreed to up front – and are appropriate when the risk to the contractor is known and manageable.

Another important point, but the government's oversight costs are also less. With a FFP contract, the contractor would typically be paid a fixed amount when they achieve a specific milestone, known simply as milestone payments. When the contractor submits an invoice for a milestone payment the oversight is minimal. Did the contractor meet the milestone? If so, issue the payment.

Cost Plus Fixed Fee (CPFF)

Again, quoting from the FAR

> A cost-plus-fixed-fee contract is a cost-reimbursement contract that provides for payment to the contractor of a negotiated fee that is fixed at the inception of the contract. The fixed fee does not vary with actual cost but may be adjusted as a result of changes in the work to be performed under the contract. This contract type permits contracting for efforts that might otherwise present too great a risk to contractors, but it provides the contractor only a minimum incentive to control costs.

If you're building more of the same widget that you delivered in the past, the risks should be well known so a FFP contract may be acceptable. But if you are trying to develop and deliver a new widget, one that delivers new capability because it uses state of the art technology that has never come to market before, the risks will be much higher. There's a risk you may not be able to get the technology to give the performance desired, in the time required, or at the cost required. A contractor would be hesitant to agree to a fixed price contract for that effort because the risk of losing money would be so great.

In those instances, a cost reimbursement contract may be more appropriate. The government would agree to reimburse the contractor's costs, plus a smaller fee, for the work provided. In this case there is more risk to the government – the contractor may require more money, more time, or may not deliver the desired capability. At the same time, there is essentially no financial risk to the contractor. They will get their costs reimbursed in full.

One brief aside before we move on. But you shouldn't be surprised to find that your program manager has radically different views on whether or not the engineering team taking on additional work, depending on the contractual vehicle.

If you're on a FFP type contract, and the engineer asks "This additional piece of work really doesn't have to be done, but it would be nice to add in this feature while we're at it. Should I do it?" Expect the PM to say "No. If it isn't required, don't do it." Why? Because you won't get paid any more for the extra effort. Saying no controls costs and maximizes profits.

If you're on a CPFF type contract and the engineer asks the same question, the PM would probably say "If it's within scope, and it won't put us over our spending limit, go ahead." Why? Because you're getting reimbursed for every hour you spend, and if you spend more hours you get paid for the extra effort. Saying yes maximizes profits.

As you can appreciate, there might be a temptation on a CPFF contract for the contractor to expand the scope of the effort a bit, so they can charge more money. To make sure the contractor really is doing value added work, the Government has to provide a lot more oversight to a CPFF project. Much more regular, and more in depth, review of the progress being made. Also, because there are no milestone payments, and instead the contractor is being reimbursed for all costs, the amount of money to be paid will likely vary from month to month, requiring more oversight from the financial team as well. There are a lot more factors that weigh in the decision to award FFP vs CPFF than we've alluded to here, and the FAR provides a lot of additional insight for those that want to dig deeper.

In our experience, FFP and CPFF (or similar cost reimbursement contracts) are the majority of the contract types you will encounter. However, two others are seen regularly, so need to be understood as well. These are Time & Material (T&M) and Indefinite Delivery Indefinite Quantity (IDIQ).

Time & Material

Quoting from the FAR

> A time-and-materials contract may be used only when it is not possible at the time of placing the contract to estimate accurately the extent or duration of the work or to anticipate costs with any reasonable degree of confidence.

The first time you see that description it might seem a little odd. Why would I want to put you under contract to do something if I couldn't accurately articulate what I wanted you to do and when? But consider the case of a service and support contract. Let's say that we delivered to the Government a new fleet of vehicles for the Army. Like any vehicle, at some point it's going to need preventive maintenance, and something will eventually break, and it will need repair. We can estimate what preventive maintenance is required, and when, and train Army personnel to do that, so it's easier to estimate that cost. But we won't be sure what might break, or when, or how expensive it would be to make the repair. Also, it might make more sense to let the people that designed and built the vehicle make the repair, rather than train Army personnel to do things they would do very infrequently. To handle those cases, a T&M contract may be more appropriate. When something breaks, I'll give you a call and authorize you to make the repair, on a T&M basis. Once the repair is done, you stop working.

That makes sense, but another question we something hear is – why doesn't the Government just wait until the vehicle breaks and issue the contract then? The answer is that oftentimes, it can take weeks or months to get a new Government contract in place because of all the checks and balances in the system. It doesn't make sense to wait until something breaks and start the contracting process. If we know something will break eventually, let's go ahead and get the contract in place now so that we won't have to wait to start the repair.

Indefinite Delivery Indefinite Quantity (IDIQ)

As with T&M, the desire to get an indefinite delivery contract in place is to enable a quicker turnaround time. Quoting from the FAR

> An (indefinite-delivery) indefinite-quantity contract provides for an indefinite quantity, within stated limits, of supplies or services during a fixed period. The Government places orders for individual requirements. Quantity limits may be stated as number of units or as dollar values

An example of a type of IDIQ contract that might be required would be for spare parts for our fleet of vehicles. We know we will need to order new tires, new windshield wipers, etc., but we aren't sure exactly when we will need them. With an IDIQ contract in place, the Government can call up the supplier and place an order for a specific quantity of items very quickly. Without the IDIQ contractual vehicle, the same process would be delayed for weeks or months while the contract was negotiated and put in place.

Subchapter D, Part 19 – Small Business Programs

One additional topic worth of note is that of small businesses. To prevent the larger companies from gaining a monopoly, and to stimulate the growth of smaller businesses, US Government contracts often have a requirement that a certain percentage of the work go to a "small business". The different small business categories are:

- Small Business (SB)
- Small Disadvantaged Business (SDB)
- Woman Owned Small Business (WOSB)
- Veteran Owned Small Business (VOSB)
- Service Disabled Veteran Owned Small Business (SDVOSB)
- Historically Underutilized Business Zone (HUBZ)

On larger procurements, which might require the capabilities of a larger firm with broader and deeper capabilities, the contractor must often document the fact that the required percentage of the work is being subcontracted to small businesses. The work does not necessarily have to be explicitly on the program in question but must meet the required cost threshold. Because showing compliance on a future procurement may be challenging, larger companies sometimes subcontract some ongoing services such as security or janitorial work to smaller companies as a means of having an ongoing small business base to build from. This is often documented in a small business subcontracting plan that may be required on US Government proposals.

All of this review of the FAR was intended to explain how the US Government buys stuff. We've looked at the specific laws and regulations, but let's take a step back and look at the broader process. In the long term, the government has to have a plan to make major purchases, and ensure they're in the budget, so we'll look at the budgeting and planning process. In the short term, there is a formal procurement process, with a fair amount of oversight so the government can assure the tax payers that the procurement was done fairly, and that the tax payers are getting the best value for their tax dollars.

BUDGETING & PLANNING

We saw in the previous chapter that most companies have a long term Strategic & Financial Plan (S&FP) and a short term Annual Operating Plan (AOP). These plans detail what business the company expects to win, and also what they plan to spend their discretionary budget (e.g., IR&D, B&P, ...) on. Most governments do similar things, but they use a different terminology. Strictly speaking, Government offices don't "win new business", but they do get allocated money that they can spend on paying their employees, contracting for new purchases, and so on. Most governments construct a long-range spending plan, similar to an S&FP, and then are allocated a specific budget for the next year, similar to an AOP. As an example of how this works, we'll look at US Government's budgeting and planning cycle.

As specified in its Constitution, the US Government is divided into three branches – legislative, executive, and judicial. The legislative branch, composed of the House of Representatives and Senate (which collectively are called Congress), makes laws. The Judicial branch, composed of the Supreme Court and other Federal Courts, evaluates the laws. The Executive Branch, composed of the President, Vice-President, and Cabinet members, enforce the laws. At the present time there are fifteen (15) Cabinet members as shown below, in order of succession to the Presidency:

- Department of State
- Department of the Treasury
- Department of Defense
- Department of Justice
- Department of the Interior
- Department of Agriculture
- Department of Commerce
- Department of Labor
- Department of Health and Human Services
- Department of Housing and Urban Development

- Department of Transportation
- Department of Energy
- Department of Education
- Department of Veterans Affairs
- Department of Homeland Security

Supporting each department, and other branches of the Government, are literally hundreds of other agencies like the Environmental Protection Agency (EPA) and the National Aeronautics and Space Administration (NASA). The thousands of federal employees all have one thing in common – they expect to get paid when they show up to work – and that means there has to be a budget so that each government organization knows what it can afford to do and plans accordingly.

The US Budget and Accounting Act of 1921 requires the President to submit a budget to Congress for each fiscal year. The US fiscal year is the 12-month period beginning on October 1 and ending on September 30 of the next calendar year. The budget must include funding requests for all federal executive departments and independent agencies.

The President's budget request is just the start of the process. The budget does not become law until:

- The House and Senate pass budget resolutions

- House and Senate Appropriations subcommittees "markup" appropriations bills

- The House and Senate vote on appropriations bills and reconcile differences

- The President signs the appropriations bill

Note that there is no obligation for either or both Houses of Congress to pass a budget resolution, and this is where the process can look rather dysfunctional.[6] If no new budget is established, the previous year's resolution remains in force. This allows existing programs to continue but can prevent the start of new programs until the new budget is agreed upon. The approval process is supposed to work as shown in Figure 11.

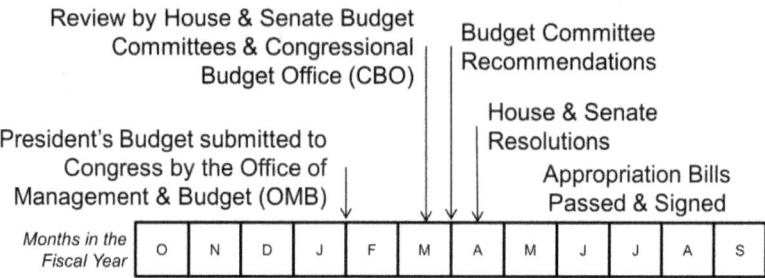

Figure 11. The US Government Budget Approval Process.

By February, the president submits a budget to the Office of Management & Budget (OMB). The House and Senate committees review and make recommendations by April, and the House and Senate begin approving the budget through a series of twelve (12) separate appropriations bills. If the process works as intended, each appropriations bill is approved before the end of the current fiscal year so that the government spending can transition smoothly to the next year. If there is a great deal of disagreement, as can often happen when the President is from one party and the House and / or Senate majority is from the other party, the process bogs down. The House and Senate may fund a series of continuing resolutions – to formally continue spending at the prior amounts – or if not approved, the government may "shut down" and send home "non-essential" employees.

---

[6] The US Congress has managed to pass all its required appropriations measures on time on only four occasions – fiscal 1977, 1989, 1995 and 1997.

The twelve (12) separate annual appropriation bills that must be approved are:

- Agriculture, Rural Development, and Food and Drug Administration
- Commerce, Justice, and Science
- Defense
- Energy and Water Development
- Financial Services and General Government
- Homeland Security
- Interior and Environment
- Labor, Health and Human Services, and Education
- Legislative Branch
- Military Construction and Veterans Affairs
- State and Foreign Operations
- Transportation and Housing and Urban Development

It can take a bit of searching to figure out where your favorite government organization receives their funding. For example, the funding for the Federal Aviation Administration (FAA) is in the Transportation and Housing and Urban Development bill, while the funding for the National Aeronautics and Space Administration (NASA) is in the Commerce, Justice, and Science bill.

The latest US budget, for FY2017, (with actuals for the prior years and projections for future years), is shown in Table 19. As can be seen, the outlays exceed the receipts by $612B. This is the yearly deficit that is contributing to the nation's total debt, estimated at over $20 Trillion at the beginning of 2018. Given the nation's population of about 323 million, that equates to a debt of over $50k per person.

As seen in Table 19, the Defense budget is the largest source of discretionary spending for the US Government, almost as large as all other sources of discretionary spending combined. The DoD is a key customer for many manufacturers in the US aerospace and defense market, so we'll take a look at its budgeting process in more detail.

Table 19. The US Government Budget for 2017. (Source – US Government Publishing Office)

In billions of dollars

	2015	2016	2017	2018	2019
Outlays					
Appropriated					
Defense	583	595	601	638	666
Non-Defense	581	627	614	626	638
Mandatory					
Social Security	882	924	967	1,025	1,089
Medicare	540	589	602	611	674
Medicaid	350	367	377	398	424
Other	529	608	629	647	692
Net Interest	223	240	304	390	473
Other	-	2	(5)	(65)	(88)
Total Outlays	**3,688**	**3,952**	**4,089**	**4,270**	**4,568**
Receipts					
Income Taxes					
Individual	1541	1628	1724	1793	1878
Corporate	344	293	343	364	401
Payroll Taxes					
Social Security	770	798	827	864	899
Medicare	234	244	253	264	276
Unemployment	51	50	49	46	46
Other	10	10	10	11	11
Excise Taxes	98	97	86	105	106
Estate and Gift Taxe	19	21	22	24	25
Customs Duties	35	37	40	42	44
Other	148	158	123	102	97
Total Receipts	**3,250**	**3,336**	**3,477**	**3,615**	**3,783**
Deficit	**(438)**	**(616)**	**(612)**	**(655)**	**(785)**

The US DoD starts thinking about its budget needs a full two and a half years before the current budget cycle as shown in Figure 12. That is, it makes an estimate of how much money it needs to fulfil its mission, and then adjusts its request based on what it thinks it will actually get, before the budget for the current year is approved. This approval process introduces several key terms that are used in the US aerospace and defense industry.

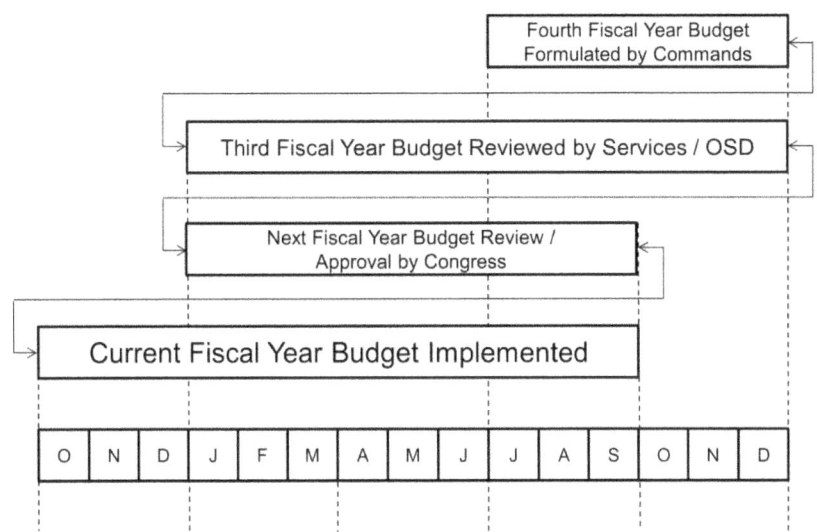

Figure 12. The US DoD Budget Cycle.

Future Years Defense Program (FYDP)

Summarizes forces, resources and equipment associated with all DoD programs.

Program Objective Memorandum (POM)

Recommendation from the Services and Defense Agencies to the Secretary of Defense concerning how they plan to allocate resources for a program to meet the Service Program Guidance (SPG) and Defense Planning Guidance (DPG).

Program of Record (PoR)

A program that has survived the POM, is included in the FYDP, and has been assigned a PE number.

Program Element (PE)

The primary data element in the FYDP and normally the

smallest aggregation of resources controlled by the Office of the Secretary of Defense (OSD). An example of a PE for a project managed by the Defense Advanced Research Projects Agency (DARPA) is shown in Figure 13.

Two important points to getting DoD funding approved are:

- If there's not a Program of Record (POR) to fund it, it won't happen; and

- It has to be in the Program Objective Memorandum (POM) before it becomes a POR

Just remember that the POM is only a projection, and there are several opportunities for the funding to disappear before it becomes a POR.

UNCLASSIFIED

Defense Advanced Research Projects Agency • President's Budget Submission FY 2016 • RDT&E Program

Program Element Table of Contents (by Budget Activity then Line Item Number)

Budget Activity 01: Basic Research
Appropriation 0400: Research, Development, Test & Evaluation, Defense-Wide

Line Item	Budget Activity	Program Element Number	Program Element Title	Page
2	01	0601101E	DEFENSE RESEARCH SCIENCES	Volume 1 – 1
4	02	0601117E	BASIC OPERATIONAL MEDICAL SCIENCE	Volume 1 – 53

Budget Activity 02: Applied Research
Appropriation 0400: Research, Development, Test & Evaluation, Defense-Wide

Line Item	Budget Activity	Program Element Number	Program Element Title	Page
9	01	0602115E	DEFENSE RESEARCH SCIENCES	Volume 1 – 1
12	02	0602303E	BASIC OPERATIONAL MEDICAL SCIENCE	Volume 1 – 53
13	02	0602304E	COGNITIVE COMPUTING SYSTEMS	Volume 1 – 107
14	02	0602383E	BIOLOGICAL WARFARE DEFENSE	Volume 1 – 113
18	02	0602702E	TACTICAL TECHNOLOGY	Volume 1 – 117
19	02	0602715E	MATERIALS AND BIOLOGICAL TECHNOLOGY	Volume 1 – 147
20	02	0602716E	ELECTRONICS TECHNOLOGY	Volume 1 - 167

UNCLASSIFIED

Volume 1 - xxiii

Figure 13. Example Program Element Listing from the US DoD Budget.

Of course, once it becomes a POR, there is still a lengthy life cycle that the POR may evolve through. This life cycle is shown in Figure 14. Many of the terms DoD suppliers use –

such as Engineering & Manufacturing Development (EMD); Low Rate Initial Production (LRIP); or Full Rate Production (FRP) – tie back to the DoD life cycle process.

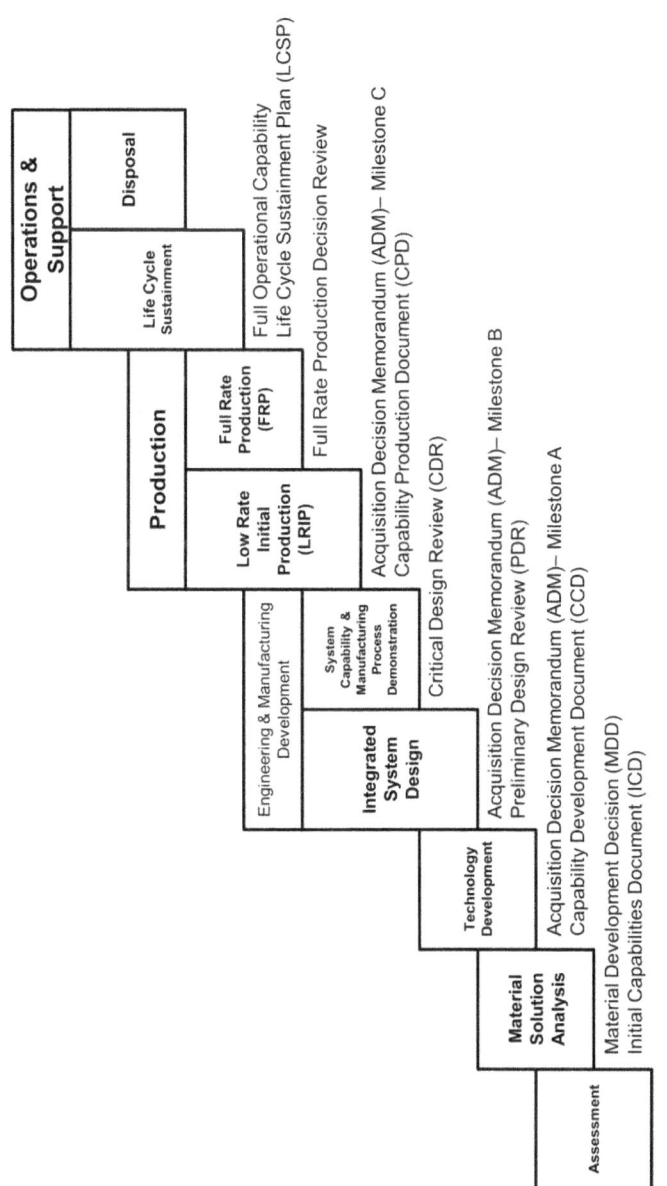

Figure 14. The DoD Project Life Cycle.

GOVERNMENT PURCHASING METHODOLOGY

After all of this review of Government Laws and Regulations, it probably comes as no surprise that the US Government, and DoD in particular, is very "regulated" about how it goes about purchasing new goods and services from companies. Again, we'll over simplify it enough to make our contracts manager uneasy but will discuss a few important points to make sure we introduce the terminology.

Request for Information (RFI)

A request for information is intended to gather insight about the capabilities of various suppliers. After we realize "I need a new widget that can do the following ...", we naturally start to ask "I wonder what's possible, and how much it would cost?" (This is the first step, Assessment, in the DoD process shown in Figure 14.)

To gather input to help answer that question the first step is often RFI. The issuing organization makes it clear that they're looking for "information" on what is available, how much it might cost, how long would it take to build, and so on. Qualified bidders are asked to provide their input.

Most of the time, qualified bidders will jump at the chance to provide information on their recommended approach, as they hope it will influence the next step, a formal Request for Proposal (RFP). If I can convince you in my RFI response that you really need a blue widget, (and not a red one, those aren't as nice as blue), and that you need to expect to pay $1M each for them, and wait 24 months for them to be delivered, AND you then plan on that going forward, that's a good day for me. When the RFP comes out and you ask for blue widgets, that have a 24-month lead time, and a cost about $1M, I'm feeling pretty good about myself. I may have successfully shaped the requirements and improved my chance of winning after I respond to the RFP.

Of course, all of the other bidders are doing very similar things. They're suggesting that yellow widgets, (not blue or red), are the way to go, and that they cost $1.2M each, but can be delivered in 18 months; and so on. The agency receiving the RFI responses is looking for common themes – is everyone telling me it takes at least 18 months to build a new widget? If so, then I should expect it to take at least that long. Is everyone telling me that widgets are about $1M each? If so, then I should expect it to cost that much.

There's no guarantee that after an RFI, you will be asked to submit a formal bid, but often times that is the case.

Request for Proposal (RFP)

An RFP, or equivalently a Request for Quote (RFQ) or Request for Tender (RFT), is a formal request for an organization to submit a legally binding bid. In general, an RFP alerts potential suppliers that the agency intends to purchase something; details the requirements for the item(s) they wish to purchase; and explains the evaluation criteria that the agency will use to select a supplier.

It may come as no surprise, but an RFP issued by a US Government agency must follow a specific format, all specified in the FAR. (To be specific, in Title 48 → Chapter 1 → Subchapter C → Part 15.) The key parts are:

- Section A – Information to Offerors or Quoters
- Section B – Supplies or Services and Price / Costs
- Section C – Statement of Work (SOW)
- Section D – Packages and Markings
- Section E – Inspection and Acceptance
- Section F – Deliveries and Performance
- Section G – Contract Administrative Data
- Section H – Special Contract Requirements
- Section I – Contract Clauses / General Provisions
- Section J – Attachments / Exhibits

- Section K – Representations / Certifications and Statements of Offerors
- Section L – Proposal Preparation Instructions, and Other
- Section M – Evaluation Criteria

Now if you remember back to our discussion of the contracts group in *Navigating the Corporation*, one of the reasons they're around is to help you wade through all of this information and make sure the bid you ultimately submit will be compliant with the requirements. As an engineer, the three elements you're most interested in are probably:

Statement of Work (SOW) – Section C

This is the section that describes exactly what the buying organization intends to buy. It lists out the specific requirements, schedule, acceptance criteria, etc. This is the foundational document that each bidder will be expected to comply with. If you can't meet one of the requirements, you're expected to point that out. Oftentimes, if you can't meet a requirement, and building the capability to meet it is too expensive, or will take too long, you may decide not to bid on the work at all. If you think you can meet the requirements, then may be able to put in a compliant proposal.

Proposal Preparation Instructions – Section L

As the title implies, this is the section that spells out what format your proposal needs to meet. It tells you how many pages you have to explain the benefits of what you're offering. Many times, the technical information must be in a separate document from the cost information. The people who are evaluating your technical approach don't need to know what it costs. They are only focusing on whether or not the approach you're describing really will work. Similarly, the people reviewing your costs aren't going to need to know the gory details of your technical proposal, but they are going to determine if your costs are "reasonable". They want to make sure you have included all the costs, and haven't overlooked anything important, especially if the agency expects to award a CPFF contract. It would look very bad to award you a contract for $1M, only to realize that after they paid you the $1M you had only finished half the work and it was really going to cost $2M.

Evaluation Criteria – Section M

This is the section that explains how they intend to evaluate your proposal. It lists explicitly what the various criteria are, and how important. It will explain how important technical is, vs cost and schedule, and it will often explain additional details about how each area will be further evaluated. For example, the technical evaluation may look for four areas, such as:

- Technical Approach to Sample Task
- Key Personnel, Management Approach, Organization and Staffing
- Relevant Experience
- Relevant Past Performance

One other thing to bear in mind in DoD procurements is the Truth In Negotiations Act (TINA). This is buried in the US Code in Title 10, which deals with the Armed Forces, Section 2306. The TINA requires bidders to provide a "certified" cost package if the threshold value is more than $750k. This is additional supporting data that substantiates why your costs are what they are. This is more work for the people in the pricing organization that have to generate that data.

Best and Final Offer (BAFO)

Sometimes, though not always, the customer may realize that they have more than one credible supplier and they find it hard to determine a clear winner based on the evaluation criteria. In those cases, the buyer may request a Best and

Final Offer (BAFO) from the short list of finalists. This is a simple request for an offer that will not be further negotiated. Sometimes, a BAFO is requested after a lengthy series of negotiations that aren't showing signs of reaching a successful conclusion rapidly. Once a BAFO is presented the buyer simply accepts or rejects it, ending negotiations.

One other reason a BAFO may be requested is because the initial analysis of the original offer may take so long, that there may be some provisions in the original proposal that are now overcome by events. The hourly rates for personnel may have changed, or material costs could have changed, so there's an opportunity to update your price. At the same time, on major procurements that are expected to take years to reach delivery, the supplier may choose to "double down" and commit discretionary spending to accelerate the schedule or mitigate risk. Requesting a BAFO gives the supplier a chance to incorporate those lessons learned in the technical proposal as well.

FISCAL AND MONETARY POLICY

In addition to protecting rights, another important thing Government's do is set fiscal and monetary policy. In economics, fiscal policy is the use of government revenue collection (mainly taxes) and expenditure (spending) to influence the economy.

We have previously discussed taxes and won't bring them up again here, other than to reiterate that tax policies can influence how people, and companies, choose to spend their money.

Governments also influence the economy by the way they spend. Government spending clearly can create some jobs – people have to build the products that the government orders – and that can influence the unemployment rate.

Closely related to fiscal policy is the concept of monetary policy. Monetary policy refers to the actions of the government central bank to influence the money supply. In the United States this responsibility falls to the Federal Reserve Bank, or simply "the Fed". When the US Congress created the Fed, via the Federal Reserve Act in 1913, the three key objectives were:

- maximize employment;
- stabilize prices; and
- moderate long-term interest rates.

Because the Federal Reserve Bank is the source of loans to many private banks, which are required to be members of the Federal Reserve System, the interest rate they charge directly influences the interest rate banks much charge to their customers. The Fed also has the authority to issue Federal Reserve Bank Notes, otherwise known as money, and controls how much money is in circulation. The value of a nation's currency, relative to all the others, is based on the amount in circulation. Increasing the amount of currency in circulation lowers its value relative to other currencies. If this happens other countries may find it more affordable to import your products, but you may find that your money buys less at home. Balancing those two extremes is a non-trivial task. We'll discuss some of the impacts of varying currency exchange rates in a future section.

CHAPTER 5
GLOBALIZATION: WORKING INTERNATIONALLY

No matter what your country of origin, it seems clear that if you want to increase the size of your addressed market, you will eventually have to break outside of your borders and expand internationally. A rough approximation of the size of each country's market – unadjusted for industry specifics – is its Gross Domestic Product (GDP) - the total value of goods produced, and services provided, in one year.

As shown in Table 20, in 2014 the US accounted for 23% of the world's total GPD of $77 trillion. The top five countries – US, China, Japan, Germany and the United Kingdom – account for half of the gross production on the planet. The next ten countries, ranked 6 thru 15, account for half of the remainder. If you want to grow your market, at some point you have to grow beyond your borders.

If your business sells to the military, the market dynamics are a bit different, but the answers are similar, as shown in Table 21. By this measure the US accounts for 36% of all worldwide military expenditures. It only takes the top three countries to exceed 50% of the world wide military expenditures; and only 7 more to account for half of the remainder. The top ten countries account for three quarters of the military spending in the world.

If you want to grow internationally you have to understand how to export from your own country and import into another. This distinction is important. Approval to leave your country of origin is only half the battle. You still need permission to arrive at your destination.

Table 20. Gross Domestic Product (GDP) for 2014. (Source: World Bank)

		Individual GDP		Cumulative GDP	
Rank	Country	$M USD	%	$M USD	%
1	United States	17,419,000	22.6%	17,419,000	22.6%
2	China	10,354,832	13.4%	27,773,832	36.0%
3	Japan	4,601,461	6.0%	32,375,293	42.0%
4	Germany	3,868,291	5.0%	36,243,584	47.0%
5	United Kingdom	2,988,893	3.9%	39,232,477	50.9%
6	France	2,829,192	3.7%	42,061,669	54.6%
7	Brazil	2,346,076	3.0%	44,407,745	57.6%
8	Italy	2,141,161	2.8%	46,548,906	60.4%
9	India	2,048,517	2.7%	48,597,423	63.1%
10	Russia	1,860,598	2.4%	50,458,021	65.5%
11	Canada	1,785,387	2.3%	52,243,408	67.8%
12	Australia	1,454,675	1.9%	53,698,083	69.7%
13	Korea, Rep.	1,410,383	1.8%	55,108,466	71.5%
14	Spain	1,381,342	1.8%	56,489,808	73.3%
15	Mexico	1,294,690	1.7%	57,784,498	75.0%
16	Indonesia	888,538	1.2%	58,673,036	76.2%
17	Netherlands	879,319	1.1%	59,552,355	77.3%
18	Turkey	798,429	1.0%	60,350,784	78.3%
19	Saudi Arabia	746,249	1.0%	61,097,033	79.3%
20	Switzerland	701,037	0.9%	61,798,070	80.2%
21	Sweden	571,090	0.7%	62,369,160	80.9%
22	Nigeria	568,508	0.7%	62,937,668	81.6%
23	Poland	544,967	0.7%	63,482,635	82.3%
24	Argentina	537,660	0.7%	64,020,295	83.0%
25	Belgium	531,547	0.7%	64,551,842	83.7%
26	Norway	499,817	0.6%	65,051,659	84.3%
27	Austria	436,888	0.6%	65,488,547	84.9%
28	Iran	425,326	0.6%	65,913,873	85.5%
29	Thailand	404,824	0.5%	66,318,697	86.0%
30	United Arab Emirates	399,451	0.5%	66,718,148	86.5%

Table 21. Military Expenditures for 2014.
(Source – World Bank)

Rank	Country	% GDP	Individual Spending $M USD	%	Cumulative Spending $M USD	%
1	United States	3.50%	$609,914	36%	$609,914	36%
2	China	2.09%	$216,427	13%	$826,341	48%
3	Russia	4.55%	$84,606	5%	$910,948	53%
4	Saudi Arabia	10.82%	$80,762	5%	$991,710	58%
5	France	2.20%	$62,286	4%	$1,053,996	61%
6	United Kingdom	2.02%	$60,440	4%	$1,114,436	65%
7	India	2.43%	$49,824	3%	$1,164,260	68%
8	Germany	1.20%	$46,453	3%	$1,210,713	71%
9	Japan	1.00%	$45,798	3%	$1,256,511	73%
10	Korea, Rep.	2.60%	$36,682	2%	$1,293,193	75%
11	Brazil	1.34%	$31,536	2%	$1,324,730	77%
12	Italy	1.44%	$30,908	2%	$1,355,637	79%
13	Australia	1.78%	$25,894	2%	$1,381,531	81%
14	United Arab Emirates	5.70%	$22,755	1%	$1,404,286	82%
15	Turkey	2.20%	$17,549	1%	$1,421,835	83%
16	Canada	0.98%	$17,450	1%	$1,439,285	84%
17	Israel	5.20%	$15,909	1%	$1,455,194	85%
18	Colombia	3.46%	$13,054	1%	$1,468,248	86%
19	Spain	0.92%	$12,732	1%	$1,480,980	86%
20	Algeria	5.56%	$11,863	1%	$1,492,843	87%
21	Poland	1.93%	$10,501	1%	$1,503,344	88%
22	Netherlands	1.15%	$10,086	1%	$1,513,430	88%
23	Singapore	3.20%	$9,840	1%	$1,523,270	89%
24	Oman	11.76%	$9,623	1%	$1,532,892	89%
25	Iraq	4.26%	$9,520	1%	$1,542,412	90%
26	Mexico	0.67%	$8,663	1%	$1,551,076	90%
27	Pakistan	3.44%	$8,387	0%	$1,559,463	91%
28	Indonesia	0.79%	$7,021	0%	$1,566,483	91%
29	Norway	1.36%	$6,776	0%	$1,573,259	92%
30	Sweden	1.15%	$6,574	0%	$1,579,833	92%

If you've ever traveled internationally you're probably familiar with the fact that you need a passport to leave your country and enter another. Depending on your country of origin, and your destination, you may also need a visa to enter the destination country. When you apply for a visa you can expect to be asked a number of questions about the purpose of your visit – are you going to visit relatives, spend some time at a resort on a vacation, or conduct business? How long will you stay? Do you have medical insurance? If not, who do you expect to pay the bills if you get sick and wind up in the hospital? Oh, and – have you been to any countries that are experiencing exotic epidemics recently? Have you been vaccinated against a long list of diseases?

If you have to answer a lot of questions just to go for a short holiday, imagine how many questions you might have to answer to permanently import your product. In the sections that follow we will examine the US export regulations that control the export of products from the United States.

US EXPORT REGULATIONS

The United States has two separate regulations, both part of the US Code of Federal Regulations discussed previously. The Export Administration Regulations (EAR) is the list of commercial products that are restricted by the Department of Commerce. The International Traffic in Arms Regulations (ITAR) is the list of military products that are restricted by the Department of State. ITAR is the more restrictive of the two, so we'll examine it first.

We should also note that having two separate sets of regulations to deal with has proven to be cumbersome, and the US Government has acknowledged that they need to merge the two into a single set of export regulations. These new regulations are expected to come out in the near future, but for now ITAR and EAR are separate.

INTERNATIONAL TRAFFIC IN ARMS REGULATIONS (ITAR)

The ITAR is part of Title 22 of the US Code of Federal Regulations, on Foreign Relations. Dig into Chapter 1 of Title 22, which deals with the Department of State, and you will see that this is where the regulations regarding visas, nationality and passports, diplomacy, and so on are found.

Subchapter M of Chapter 1 is the ITAR, which is further broken down into various parts as shown in Table 22. The key parts for manufacturers are Parts 121, 123, 124, and 125. We'll examine each of these briefly.

Table 22. International Traffic in Arms Regulations (ITAR).

Part	Title
120	Purposes and Definitions
121	The United States Munitions List
122	Registration of Manufacturers and Exporters
123	Licenses for the Export of Defense Articles
124	Agreements, Off-Shore Procurement and Other Defense Services
125	Licenses for the Export of Technical Data and Classified Defense Articles
126	General Policies and Provisions
127	Violations and Penalties
128	Administrative Procedures
129	Registration and Licensing of Brokers
130	Political Contributions, Fees and Commissions

Part 120 – The United States Munition List

The United States Munition List (USML) is broken into twenty-one categories as shown in Table 23. When you dig into the details of a specific category or section you will find the limitations on what can, and cannot, be exported without authorization from the Department of State. For example, in Category VIII – Aircraft and Associated Equipment, it clarifies that any aircraft that are designed specifically for military purposes are indeed controlled by ITAR.

Table 23. Part 121 – United States Munitions List (USML).

Category	Title
I	Firearms, Close Assault Weapons, and Combat Shotguns
II	Guns and Armament
III	Ammunition / Ordnance
IV	Launch Vehicles, Guided Missiles, Ballistic Missiles, Rockets, Torpedoes, Bombs, and Mines
V	Explosives and Energetic Materials, Propellants, Incendiary Agents and Their Constituents
VI	Vessels of War and Special Naval Equipment
VII	Tanks and Military Vehicles
VIII	Aircraft and Associated Equipment
IX	Military Training Equipment and Training
X	Protective Personnel Equipment and Shelters
XI	Military Electronics
XII	Fire Control, Range Finders, Optical and Guidance and Control Equipment
XIII	Auxiliary Military Equipment
XIV	Toxicological Agents, Including Chemical Agents, Biological Agents, and Associated Equipment
XV	Spacecraft Systems and Associated Equipment
XVI	Nuclear Weapons, Design and Testing Related Items
XVII	Classified Articles, Technical Data and Defense Services Not Otherwise Enumerated
XVIII	Directed Energy Weapons
XIX	Reserved
XX	Submersible Vessels, Oceanographic and Associated Equipment
XXI	Miscellaneous Articles

Quoting straight from the first lines of Category VIII, ITAR restricted equipment includes:

a) Aircraft, as follows:

(1) Bombers;

(2) Fighters, fighter bombers, and fixed-wing attack aircraft;

(3) Turbofan- or turbojet-powered trainers used to train pilots for fighter, attack, or bomber aircraft;

(4) Attack helicopters;

(5) Unarmed military unmanned aerial vehicles (UAVs)

(6) Armed unmanned aerial vehicles (UAVs)

(7) Military intelligence, surveillance, and reconnaissance aircraft;

(8) Electronic warfare, airborne warning and control aircraft;

(9) Air refueling aircraft;

(10) Target drones

Reading through the gory details of the ITAR is not very enlightening and we don't intend to dig further into it here. But the point is, if you are exporting equipment that is on the USML it is your responsibility to figure out what portions of the USML are applicable and apply for a license. The type of licenses that may be required are in Part 123.

Part 123 – Defense Article Licenses

Any organization who intends to export, or to import temporarily, a defense article must obtain the approval of the Office of Defense Trade Controls. The types of licenses that may be required are listed in Table 24. It is important to note that licenses are very specific. They are authorized by part number, not just general capability. Also, once the export of the article is approved, that includes only the article itself, and not any other data or services that might be required to effectively understand how to use the article. That data is covered in Part 124.

Table 24. Part 123 – Defense Article Licenses.

License	Title
DSP-5	Application for Permanent Export of Unclassified Defense Articles, Related Technical Data, and Defense Services (aka Permanent Export License or PEL)
DSP-61	Application/License for Temporary Import of Unclassified Defense Articles (aka Temporary Import License or TIL)
DSP-73	Application/License for Temporary Export of Unclassified Defense Articles (aka Temporary Export License or TEL)
DSP-85	Application for Permanent/Temporary Export or Temporary Import of Classified Defense Articles and Related Classified Technical Data
DSP-94	Authority to Export Defense Articles Sold under the Foreign Military Sales Program

Part 124 – Agreements, Off-Shore Procurement, and Other Defense Services

The Office of Defense Trade Controls must also approve the transfer of defense services. These agreements are generally characterized as either:

- Manufacturing License Agreements (MLA)
    o Required if you want to set up a manufacturing capability in the country

- Technical Assistance Agreements (TAA)
    o Required if you want to transfer data or provide technical assistance

- Distribution Agreement (DA), or
- Off-Shore Procurement Agreements

Additional insight on the regulations covering export of technical data are in Part 125.

Part 125 – Licenses for the Export of Technical Data and Classified Defense Articles

You need an export if you want to export technical data from the United States. Specifically, you need a Technical Data License (TDL) – DSP-5 – if you want to share data (knowledge) with

- A foreign national (e.g., a citizen of another country)
    o Even if the foreign national is in the US legally

- A US citizen that is employed by a foreign owned company

Note also that every time you export data, you are expected to go back to the site hosted by the DoS and confirm that it's still okay to export to the company on the TDL. Things change, and you – as the exporter of record – have the obligation to continue to check for updates.

The bottom line on ITAR is that if you discover the product or service you want to provide is on the USML, you must apply for a TAA or TDL that would give you permission to transfer data on your product to the foreign national or foreign company. (Remember, even a US citizen employed by a foreign owned company is considered an export.) If you want to take the product over to a trade show or to do an integration fit check, but intend to bring the product back home again, then you need a Temporary Export License (TEL). Once the TEL is approved it will be for a very specific purpose. You probably can't go to a trade show and decide to stay and do an integration check, it's typically one or the other. Then before you make final delivery you will need a Permanent Export License (PEL).

We should note that the ITAR governs the Direct Commercial Sale (DCS) of military equipment from a private company to another company or government. A government to government transaction is known as a Foreign Military Sale (FMS). In the case of an FMS, your customer would be the US Government, who in turn provides the article or service to the foreign Government. In those cases, strictly speaking your company is not making the export, but the US Government is. That simplifies the ITAR paperwork a bit, at the expense of an equally cumbersome process as follows.

The Arms Export Control Act (AECA) authorizes the sale of defense articles and services to foreign countries and international organizations when the sale will strengthen the security of the US and promote world peace. The FMS is a government-to-government sales agreement and may be funded by country national funds or US Government funds. This is similar to, but distinct from, Foreign Military Financing (FMF) which is a US grant or loan to enable purchase of US defense articles, services, or training. The process for an FMS is shown in Figure 15.

As shown, the first step is a formal Letter of Request (LOR) from the foreign government to the US government asking the US to provide the product in question. Often there are two steps here – after the first LOR the US Government asks the manufacture to provide a quote for pricing and availability. In other words, how much would it cost and how long would it take to deliver?

Once the numbers are understood and agreed to, the final LOR is submitted for approval. At this point the Department of State takes over and, after working with Congress, eventually generates a Letter of Acceptance that confirms what the US is agreeing to provide. Then, the foreign government provides the funding, and the US military writes a formal RFP, gets a quote, and places a purchase order with the vendor. The vendor then builds and delivers the product to a freight forwarder. The freight forwarder, or shipper, then follows an expedited process to get the export license, the DSP-94, in place and delivers the product.

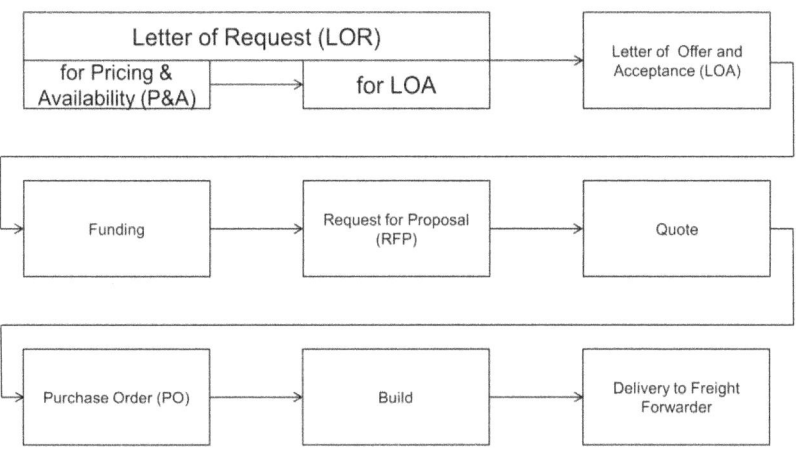

Figure 15. The Process of Completing a Foreign Military Sale.

If the product is not on the USML and not restricted by the ITAR, the product may still be restricted by the Department of Commerce via the Export Administration Regulations (EAR), so you must be familiar with both sets of regulations.

EXPORT ADMINISTRATION REGULATIONS (EAR)

The EAR is in Title 15 – Commerce and Foreign Trade, Subtitle B – Regulations Relating to Commerce and Foreign Trade, Subchapter C. The EAR regulates the export and re-export of most commercial items. The Department of Commerce's Bureau of Industry and Security (BIS) is responsible for implementing and enforcing the EAR.

Similar to the ITAR, where you needed to determine if the item was on the USML and its category, for the EAR you will need to determine if the item is on the Commerce Control List (CCL) and the items Export Control Classification Number (ECCN).

The ECCN is an alpha-numeric code that is listed in the CCL. Each item has a specific ECCN. The format uses the convention:

> (Category) (Group) (###)

The categories are defined in Table 25, and the groups are defined in Table 26. For example, if your product is seen to be in:

> Category 3 – Electronics
>
> Group A – Equipment, Assemblies and Components

The US DoC would then assign a unique identifier, something like 123. In this example, the ECCN would be 3A123.

In our experience, when you export something – even if you are just temporarily exporting it for an onsite demonstration, you must laboriously determine the ECCN for each and every component you plan to send. This leads to some interesting conversations with the engineering staff, when you ask their help in determining the ECCN classification of what they might consider everyday items such as Ethernet cables. Although it may very well be an everyday item to an engineer who works with computers, the clerk at the customs office probably won't have an engineering background and may not know an Ethernet cable from an HDMI cable.[7]

Table 25. EAR Export Categories.

Category	Title
0	Nuclear Materials, Facilities and Equipment and Miscellaneous
1	Materials, Chemicals, "Microorganisms," and Toxins
2	Materials Processing
3	Electronics
4	Computers
5	Telecommunications and Information Security
6	Lasers and Sensors
7	Navigation and Avionics
8	Marine
9	Propulsion Systems, Space Vehicles and Related Equipment

Table 26. EAR Export Groups.

Groups	Title
A	Equipment, Assemblies and Components
B	Test, Inspection and Production Equipment
C	Materials
D	Software
E	Technology

Rather than fight it, be prepared to go with the flow. Label everything explicitly and keep track of them once you're in country doing the demo. You'll want to count everything again before it gets packed up to ship back and make sure

---

[7] Yes, there really are people like that out there.

the numbers still add up. If your export license said you were bringing ten Ethernet cables and you only find nine of them when you're packing up to come back home, that's a potential problem. If that omission gets discovered, you set yourself up for greater scrutiny and may even have to pay a fine or importation tax for the item you left behind.

Once you know the ECCN, then you need to know if there are any export restrictions associated with the country you want to export it to. For example, if you want to export something to Canada – a longtime ally of the United States – you will probably find that the EAR is very liberal where Canada is concerned. In contrast, if you want to export the same item to North Korea – a longtime adversary of the United States – you will probably find that the EAR is very conservative. The list of items you could export to North Korea is minimal.

The bottom line with all of that is that your export control group can help you determine if the article is export restricted and what export licenses are required. Start early. Approvals take months, not days.

FOREIGN IMPORT REGULATIONS

Now that we have all of the approvals in place to export the item from the US, we're home free right? Wrong. Getting out of the US is only part of the problem. You still need to get into the country of destination.

Remember in our earlier example we talked about how you need a passport to enable yourself to travel across borders, and in some cases, you may need a visa to enter other countries. It's the same with hardware. First, you may need to get an import license that allows you to ship the article into the country. You may also have to pay duty or tax on the item when you do so.

A special case can occur when you want to only temporarily import an item, for a demonstration for example, but you plan to take it out again later before permanently importing it. When you try to import an item, you may be expected to pay a duty on the item, unless you can give assurance that the item is only being temporarily imported. A document that can help with this is called a Carnet, which is in essence a passport for hardware.

Back in the 1960s, the World Customs Organization, (then known as the Customs Cooperation Council), adopted the ATA Carnet as a process for the temporary admission of goods. (ATA is an acronym that mixes French and English terms and stands for "Admission Temporaire / Temporary Admission".) Carnet's can be used to import commercial samples, professional equipment, or goods for presentation or use at trade fairs, exhibits, etc., to many countries around the world. As of 2018, about 87 countries recognized Carnets as a means of temporarily importing goods. If you are going to temporarily import an article, you would typically be encouraged to obtain an ATA Carnet, rather than paying the importation tax. However, like a visa, a carnet has an expiration date. Make sure that you have plans to bring the item back home well in advance of the expiration date. If you forget, the item can get impounded and then you will have to pay a fine and the importation duty before you can get it back.

Often, getting the import license (or winning the contract to deliver the item) is granted only when you agree to additional conditions that apply to foreign suppliers. These laws usually only apply when a government department, (e.g., the military), purchases from a foreign supplier, and may not apply if a company purchases from a foreign supplier. The names for these practices vary, but may include

- Balances
- Equilibrium
- Industrial compensations

- Industrial cooperation
- Industrial and regional benefits
- Juste retour
- Offsets

All of these practices are based on the principle that countries would prefer to spend their tax dollars in their own country, and in those hopefully rare instances when they can't, would like to trade something for the product or service they're acquiring rather than simply outlay the cash and see it leave. For example, an offset agreement is an agreement where the company delivering the product to the foreign government agrees to buy products from the country as a condition of winning the contract. This agreement offsets the buyer's outlay of cash. The government stipulates that the seller must spend a percentage of the contract value within the country. It does not necessarily mean that a fixed percentage of the cost of the item being purchased has to be provided by subcontractors in the country. That is preferred, but if the country's suppliers had the capability to make it themselves they probably wouldn't be giving you the contract in the first place. Instead, you commit to spending a fixed dollar amount on other products provided by the country. Those could be much lower technology items like office supplies or office furniture, as long as they are manufactured locally.

Because this is not always a straight forward task, many large companies have a centralized office that manages their offset requirements. They keep track at the corporate level of what the offset obligation is in every country, and in some cases, can trade offset obligations with other companies who may have a surplus in the country of interest.

Navigating all of these unfamiliar regulations is often quite a daunting task. To make sure they are doing it right companies often hire an International Sales Representative (ISR), a local representative that understands the countries laws, culture, and language, who is the onsite representative of the company. Many countries require an approved ISR to ensure that the ISR really does understand the local laws.

The ISR is the agent that is authorized to solicit business for a firm, and is compensated through a commission, or salary, or a combination of both. They are paid to know who to talk to, what value proposition will be well received, to assist with translation into the local languages, etc. The ISRs agreement may give them a percentage of anything sold via DCS (Direct Commercial Sale) in that country. It's very important that you include this commission in your business case as it will degrade the margins a bit. Note that your ISR may not be able to assist with FMS (Foreign Military Sales). In some cases, they may be able to legally, but would be unmotivated to do so if they are unable to receive a commission on the sale. Note that the military attaché at the US Embassy often assists locally with FMS purchases, since it is a government to government transaction.

CURRENCY EXCHANGE RATES

One other significant item that you have to bear in mind when you choose to do business internationally is – what currency do you want to get paid in? If you're a US company you'd probably prefer to get paid in US dollars, but if the buyer is the Government of India they'll probably insist on paying you in their currency, Indian rupees. Again, if you've traveled internationally on personal business you're probably familiar with the need to exchange currency as you cross borders. There's a small fee for doing that, so again that has to be factored into your business case because that exchange fee erodes your margins. If the exchange rate were fixed, it would be trivially easy to calculate the cost of the exchange. But the exchange rate varies. That creates a challenge as you try to predict how the exchange rate, at some point in the future when you deliver the product and get paid, will affect your business case.

Consider for example the exchange rate between the Euro and the US Dollar as shown in Figure 16. As you can see, in July 2011 the exchange rate was about $1.00 USD = €0.70 Euro. In January 2016, it was about $1.00 USD = €0.95 Euro. What would such an exchange rate fluctuation do to your business case? As is easy to see, you could be both helped, or hurt, by the fluctuation, depending on which side of the exchange you are on.

**Figure 16. Currency Exchange Rate, US Dollars to EUROs.
(Source – www.usforex.com)**

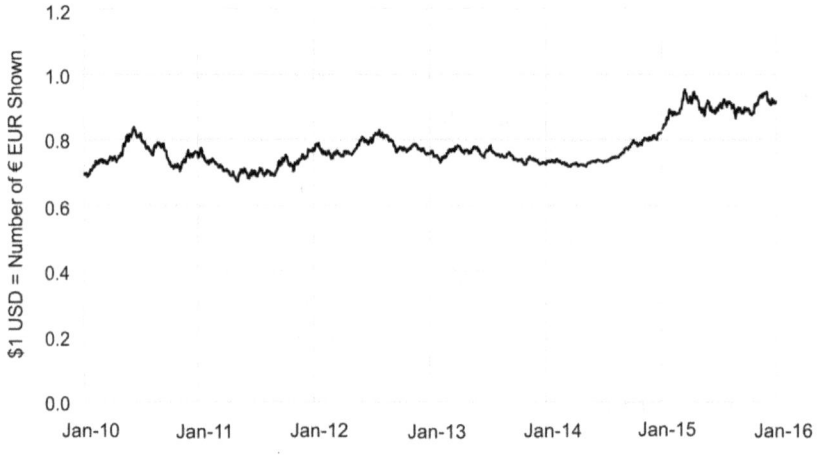

Consider the case where you signed a contract in July 2011 and agreed to get paid €100,000 upon delivery of a product you would deliver in July 2012. At contract signing, you would expect to receive €100,000 x ($1.00 USD / €0.70) = $142,847 USD. But one year later, upon delivery, the exchange rate was approximately $1.00 USD = €0.800 Euro. That would translate to an income of €100,000 x ($1.00 USD / €0.80) = $125,000 USD. The net was a loss of $17,847 USD due to currency fluctuations.

But what if the transaction went the other direction? What if you were a European supplier who agreed to get paid

$100,000 upon delivery? At contract signing, you would expect to receive $100,000 x (€0.70 / $1.00 USD) = €70,000. But one year later, upon delivery, the exchange rate was approximately $1.00 USD = €0.80 Euro. That would translate to an income of $100,000 x (€0.80 / $1.00 USD) = €80,000. The net was a gain of €10,000 due to the same currency fluctuations.

Note that if you signed the same contract one year later – agreement in July 2012 for delivery in 2013 – the results would have been reversed. A US supplier delivering to a European company would have gained money on the exchange, while a European supplier delivering to an American company would have lost money. Because most companies don't have a full staff of economic advisors to dig into the details of likely future exchange rates, they look to the full-time investors for advice. To protect against currency exchange rate fluctuations, it's possible to obtain a currency hedge to limit the risk. A hedge is basically a right to exchange currency in the future at a rate agreed to today. Of course, there's a fee for that privilege, but it limits the risk of the currency exchange rate changing beyond the agreed to rate.

Let's say that you were an American company who signed a contract for €100,000 in July 2012 and decided you wanted a hedge fund that would lock in your exchange rate at no more than $1.00 USD / €0.80. When you delivered in July 2013 the actual exchange rate was $1.00 USD / €0.85. Without the hedge you'd receive €100,000 x ($1.00 USD / €0.85) = $117,647. Because you have a hedge, you can use it and receive €100,000 x ($1.00 USD / €0.80) = $125,000, an increase of $7,353. Of course, if the exchange rate moved the other direction, to ($1.00 USD / €0.75) you wouldn't exercise the hedge and would collect the full €100,000 x ($1.00 USD / €0.75) = $133,333.

Depending on the economic forecast, you may wish to invest in a hedge to limit the risk of your business case eroding further. The cost of that hedge also needs to be factored into your business case and will further limit your margins.

Between the cost of the hedge fund, the cost of the commission to the ISR, etc., it certainly looks like working internationally has the potential to be less profitable. Often it is less profitable, but as long as it remains profitable, it's probably worth doing. If you're able to increase the size of your market by 50%, then you probably can generate some additional cash savings in your manufacturing processes by negotiating better purchase prices from your subcontractors – since you're now buying 50% more supplies than you were in the past. That indirectly makes the original business base more profitable, which further increases the bottom line.

We always remember the advice given to us by an experienced sales rep who had worked internationally for years – it will take you twice as long to make half as much money – as compared to the US. But if you have the patience to understand the foreign procurement regulations and establish a regular presence to convince the customers that they can depend on you to be there if they have a problem, it's a great way to expand your brand name and your business.

CULTURAL DIFFERENCES

We've mentioned the currency differences, which are important. But equally, if not more important, are the cultural differences. The dictionary defines culture as "a way of thinking, behaving, or working that exists in a place or organization" such as a business, or a country. Your business has a unique culture – a unique way that they present their value proposition to their customers, a unique way that they expect everybody to do things at work, and so on. Ultimately, leaders are responsible for exemplifying the culture they want out of the organization, and one of the toughest challenges for leaders is to change the culture of the organization when necessary. Edgar Schein, a Professor Emeritus with the MIT Sloan School of Management, once observed

> "... culture constrains leadership in a mature company, just as leaders create culture in a young company"

If you want to do business internationally, you have to adapt to a completely different culture. Not only could the language and currency be different, but the procurement regulations are likely different as well. We've traveled a lot to India, so we'll use that as an example.

As an American who wants to do business in India, you will probably find it's very easy to conduct business in English. After all, the English had a strong presence in India as far back as 1599 when the British East Indies Company set up shop to facilitate trade. By 1858, India ruled about 60% of India directly, and the other 40% of India indirectly followed British policies. By the time of Indian independence in 1947, most of the educated population spoke English and followed policies that looked distinctly British in origin.

Speaking the same language makes conducting business easy, but that just sets up a subtle trap. We like to assume that because someone else is speaking our language we both mean the same thing when we use the same words. That's not always the case. An American who orders biscuits for breakfast in England would be surprised when they bring out a plate of cookies.[8]

Even if we use the same word, and it means the same thing, there are often subtle cultural differences. In American culture it's not unusual to say the word "no".

> "Can you deliver the first test unit by March 1st?"

---

[8] Yes, I really did that.

> "No. There's just no way I can get it the by the 1st. The 15th is more reasonable."

In American culture it's not proper for me to mislead you and let you think the 1st is possible, if I know it isn't. I would be very straight forward in telling you "No – I can't do that". Americans are very direct communicators in that sense. We tell you directly what we're thinking.

In some cultures, it's considered impolite to use the word "no". One of my colleagues who did a lot of business in Japan once observed "This is how people in Japan tell you no". He then sat still with his mouth shut for the next 60 seconds. His point was, many other countries will avoid using that word because their culture has taught them not to use it. As Americans, we have to learn to look for the signs that they're trying to tell us "no", even though they aren't coming out and saying it directly.

In other cultures, they will use the word "no" very liberally. Instead of it meaning "I can't do it" it may simply mean "I don't want to commit to it. That would be hard, and I really don't want to disappoint you if I'm late."

We were doing a demo in India once and were given an unrealistic date for showing up and completing the tests. We said "no – we can't commit to having everything ready by that date". But our customer insisted. After some negotiation, we reluctantly agreed that since our customer told us that was the only date that was a possibility and if we didn't show up then we'd be dropped from consideration, we'd do the best we could. We showed up and completed about 90% of the tests but, as we predicted, hadn't been able to add the new features required to complete the other 10% of the tests. Our customer was shocked and observed, "But you only said no once!" In our culture, saying no once was sufficient. In their culture, the first no only meant it was painful. He expected us to continue to explain why we couldn't do it two, three, four or more times before he would accept, okay – you really can't do it, and it's not that you just don't want to.

You can also get into similar disagreements over the interpretation of "yes". Sometimes "yes" means "I will do it." In other cases, "yes" means "I understand what you want." In India we used to ask our local driver, "Will you pick us up at 8:00 am?". The answer 100% of the time was "yes". The percentage of times we were actually picked up at 8:00 am was provably zero. In this case, his "yes" just meant that he understood when we wanted to get picked up. He never intended it to be a firm commitment that he would be there at that time. We've learned that a better question is "When will you be able to pick us up tomorrow?" The answer to that question gives a much better guess as to when the car will show up to get you.

So how do you manage all of that? With the help of your International Sales Representative. They are the ones who have the responsibility for interpreting those cultural differences. You may leave a meeting thinking "They said yes to our price increase. This is great!" While your local rep will quietly remind you, "That yes only means they understand you want to increase the price. They really haven't agreed to it yet."

In addition to cultural differences, there are likely some legal differences in the process as well. As we saw in *The Rules of the Road*, the US Government follows the procedures specified in the Federal Acquisition Regulation (FAR). In India, the Government follows the Defence Procurement Procedure (DPP).

One of the key differences between the FAR and DPP, at least to us, being used to US culture, is that the American government has the concept of "best value" when it does its procurements. They might be willing to pay a bit more for your product vs mine, if you can quantify how your product is really a better value in the long run. Maybe it exceeds the technical requirements or has lower life cycle maintenance costs. If you can articulate the advantage, it may sway the decision in your favor. In India, and many other countries, they don't purchase things on the basis of "best value". They purchase them on the basis of "lowest cost, technical compliance". That is, there is a technical evaluation that simply answers the question – is the product compliant with the specification? At the end of the day you get a simple pass or fail answer. It doesn't matter if you passed all the requirements with healthy margins, or just barely cleared the bar, the result is the same – pass. You get no extra credit for exceeding the minimum requirements. All of the compliant bidders then go to the next phase, when they look at your cost. They then select the lowest cost option.

In other countries, we've been invited to the down select, which is conducted much like an auction. The person in charge will acknowledge that the vendors present are all considered compliant, so he's ready to receive your sealed bids for the cost of the contract. After reviewing them the procurement official may announce, "I'm sorry, but nobody has yet met our approved price for awarding the contract. Would you like to re-bid?" You then have a few minutes to submit a lower bid, or decide not to, and the process repeats. Eventually you will learn "One of the vendors has met our cost target. Would anybody like to submit a revised bid?" At this point, you can hope that you are the low bidder and that nobody submits a lower bid, or you can guess that you are not the low bidder and decide to submit an even lower price. Again, work with your international sales rep to make sure you understand the procurement process used locally.

CHAPTER 6

PLANNING FOR SUCCESS

I once worked for a manager who observed that if you could show somebody else's design to an engineer, and the second engineer couldn't find anything about the design they wanted to change, you just should fire them on the spot. He wasn't advocating for a Draconian style of management, he had just observed that most people go into engineering because they want to design new and exciting products, and everybody has a different opinion about how to do that. In the course of our career it's natural that we'll see opportunities for new products or new features. In this chapter, we'll talk briefly about how those ideas get turned into reality

CONCEPT DEFINITION

The view of the International Council on Systems Engineering (INCOSE) is that every system or product life cycle consists of [9]

- The technical aspect (product)
- The business aspect (business case)
- The budget aspect (funding)

The job of the systems engineer is to create technical solutions that are consistent with the business case and the funding. Let's briefly review each of these aspects.

---

[9] INCOSE Systems Engineering Handbook, INCOSE-TP-2003-002-03.1, Section 3.2.1

THE TECHNICAL ASPECT

Any plan for a new product or service starts by defining the scope of work, or technical concept for what you are proposing to do. Will you add new features to an existing product? Will you develop technologies to enable a new prototype product, or develop a complete prototype? The technical aspect is simply a description of what you plan to do, and how you plan to do it. It describes all of the work that is "in plan" for the new project.

A good way to start defining the technical scope is to answer the Heilmeier questions. George Heilmeier was a director of the US Defense Advanced Research Projects Agency (DARPA) in the 1970s. He proposed a set of questions, sometimes known as the "Heilmeier Catechism", to help evaluate proposed research programs. Those questions were:

- What are you trying to do?
- How is it done today, and what are the limits of current practice?
- What is new in your approach and why do you think it will be successful?
- Who cares? If you are successful, what difference will it make?
- What are the risks?
- How much will it cost?
- How long will it take?
- What are the mid-term and final "exams" to check for success?

If you can answer those questions, preferably in language a

teenager can understand, you should have a fairly complete description of the project you want to undertake. As you begin to think about each question individually, you will realize that they lead to more and more questions as you try to address the unknowns and ensure that the answers are all self-consistent.

Expect somebody to ask – if this is such a great idea, why hasn't somebody else done it before? Sometimes, the answer is that the technology available in the past wasn't mature enough to allow this type of product. It's important to be familiar with terms like Technology Readiness Level (TRL) or Manufacturing Readiness Level (MRL) as shown in Table 27 and Table 28, respectively. Note that different branches of the US Government use slightly different definitions for TRLs and MRLs, and these tables use the definitions recommended by the US Department of Defense (DoD).

The Technology Readiness Level is a measure of how mature the technology is. Think of an example with simple electrical parts. Are the parts in production, tested to the environmental extremes appropriate for your product, and actually used in similar products today? If so, then that technology is probably TRL 9 – an actual system (using that technology) has been proven through successful mission operations. This could be the case for a lot of readily available parts like Field Programmable Gate Arrays (FPGAs) or General Purpose Processors (GPPs) that might go into a standard personal computer or workstation.

But if you were trying to design and build a quantum computer, which could be orders of magnitude more capable, you would probably find that you couldn't buy a quantum processor. They're back up about TRL 1 – basic principles observed and reported. The first challenge could be finding a supplier for the parts you need.

Table 27. Technology Readiness Levels. (US Department of Defense)

Level	Definition	DoD TRL Description
1	Basic principles observed and reported	Lowest level of technology readiness. Scientific research begins to be translated into applied research and development. Examples might include paper studies of a technology's basic properties.
2	Technology concept and/or application formulated.	Invention begins. Once basic principles are observed, practical applications can be invented. Applications are speculative and there may be no proof or detailed analysis to support the assumptions. Examples are limited to analytic studies.
3	Analytical and experimental critical function and/or characteristic proof of concept.	Active research and development is initiated. This includes analytical studies and laboratory studies to physically validate analytical predictions of separate elements of the technology. Examples include components that are not yet integrated or representative.
4	Component and/or breadboard validation in laboratory environment	Basic technological components are integrated to establish that they will work together. This is relatively "low fidelity" compared to the eventual system. Examples include integration of "ad hoc" hardware in the laboratory.
5	Component and/or breadboard validation in relevant environment.	Fidelity of breadboard technology increases significantly. The basic technological components are integrated with reasonably realistic supporting elements so it can be tested in a simulated environment. Examples include "high fidelity" laboratory integration of components.
6	System/subsystem model or prototype demonstration in a relevant environment.	Representative model or prototype system, which is well beyond that of TRL 5, is tested in a relevant environment. Represents a major step up in a technology's demonstrated readiness. Examples include testing a prototype in a highfidelity laboratory environment or in simulated
7	System prototype demonstration in an operational environment.	Prototype near, or at, planned operational system. Represents a major step up from TRL 6, requiring demonstration of an actual system prototype in an operational environment such as an aircraft, vehicle, or space. Examples include testing the prototype in a test bed aircraft.
8	Actual system completed and qualified through test and demonstration.	Technology has been proven to work in its final form and under expected conditions. In almost all cases, this TRL repressnts the end of true system development. Examples include developmental test and evaluation of the system in its intended weapon system to determine if it meets design specifications.
9	Actual system proven through successful mission operations.	Actual application of the technology in its final form and under mission conditions, such as those encountered in operational test and evaluation. Examples include using the system under operational mission conditions.

Table 28. Manufacturing Readiness Levels. (US Department of Defense)

Level	Definition	DoD MRL Description
1	Basic Manufacturing Implications Identified	Basic research expands scientific principles that may have manufacturing implications. The focus is on a high level assessment of manufacturing opportunities. The research is unfettered.
2	Manufacturing Concepts Identified	This level is characterized by describing the application of new manufacturing concepts. Applied research translates basic research into solutions for broadly defined military needs.
3	Manufacturing Proof of Concept Developed	This level begins the validation of the manufacturing concepts through analytical or laboratory experiments. Experimental hardware models have been developed in a laboratory environment that may possess limited functionality.
4	Capability to produce the technology in a laboratory environment	This level of readiness acts as an exit criterion for the MSA Phase approaching a Milestone A decision. Technologies should have matured to at least TRL 4. This level indicates that the technologies are ready for the Technology Development Phase of acquisition. Producibility assessments of design concepts have been completed. Key design performance parameters have been identified as well as any special tooling, facilities, material handling and skills required.
5	Capability to produce prototype components in a production relevant environment	Mfg. strategy refined and integrated with Risk Management Plan. Identification of enabling/critical technologies and components is complete. Prototype materials, tooling and test equipment, as well as personnel skills have been demonstrated on components in a production relevant environment, but many manufacturing processes and procedures are still in development.
6	Capability to produce a prototype system or subsystem in a production relevant environment	This MRL is associated with readiness for a Milestone B decision to initiate an acquisition program by entering into the EMD Phase of acquisition. Technologies should have matured to at least TRL 6. The majority of manufacturing processes have been defined and characterized, but there are still significant engineering and/or design changes in the system itself.
7	Capability to produce systems, subsystems, or components in a production representative environment	System detailed design activity is nearing completion. Material specifications have been approved and materials are available to meet the planned pilot line build schedule. Manufacturing processes and procedures have been demonstrated in a production representative environment. Detailed producibility trade studies are completed and producibility enhancements and risk assessments are underway. Technologies should be on a path to achieve TRL 7.
8	Pilot line capability demonstrated; Ready to begin Low Rate Initial Production	The system, component or item has been previously produced, is in production, or has successfully achieved low rate initial production. Technologies should have matured to TRL 9. This level of readiness is normally associated with readiness for entry into Full Rate Production (FRP). All systems engineering/design requirements should have been met such that there are minimal system changes. Major system design features are stable and have been proven in test and evaluation.
9	Low rate production demonstrated; Capability in place to begin Full Rate Production.	The system, component or item has been previously produced, is in production, or has successfully achieved low rate initial production. Technologies should have matured to TRL 9. This level of readiness is normally associated with readiness for entry into Full Rate Production (FRP). All systems engineering/design requirements should have been met such that there are minimal system changes.
10	Full Rate Production demonstrated and lean production practices in place	Technologies should have matured to TRL 9. This level of manufacturing is normally associated with the Production or Sustainment phases of the acquisition life cycle. Engineering/design changes are few and generally limited to quality and cost improvements. System, components or items are in full rate production and meet all engineering, performance, quality and reliability requirements. Manufacturing process capability is at the appropriate quality level.

A similar story is true for the Manufacturing Readiness Level. At MRL 1 – basic manufacturing implications identified, you may be able to understand at a very high level how your company's factory would have to change to convert it over to building your new product. However, that's a far cry from MRL 10 – already being in full rate production.[10]

The point is, just because you can conceive of it, doesn't mean you can actually build a prototype, or mature the prototype into a product that you would stand behind with a warranty. Oftentimes researchers in academia focus on state of the art technology or manufacturing at the lower TRL / MRL values, while mass production requires very high TRL / MRL values.

THE BUSINESS CASE

Even before we have the concept for a new product or service thoroughly defined, we'll want to start working on the business case. The business case is the financial reason for doing the technical work. In some cases, the business case may be simple. If the Government enacts a new law that requires you to add new features to your products, or you won't be able to continue to sell them, it's an all or nothing proposition. If we don't invest $X to add the new features, our revenue stream will drop to zero. But most of the time, the business case is not so simple. If we invest $X to add in new features, will we be able to sell more units, and at a higher price?

So, if we can define what we want to do (technical aspect) the next step is to determine how much it's going to cost and why it will be worth doing. That is the business case.

A business case does two things – it qualifies and quantifies your value proposition. That is, it explains what you plan to do – the work you plan to accomplish, the features you will

---

[10] Terms like Full Rate Production are part of the DoD Life Cycle terminology as shown in Figure 20.

add to a product, etc. – and it also quantifies that value. It specifies how much better the new product will be versus the old. Note that there may be two aspects to this problem – internal and external. If you're developing a product for an external customer – if you're proposing that they fund the development, or just buy the new product at the end of the day – they are not going to care a lot about your internal cost structure. They're going to care about the new feature set – the new value the product brings – and will make a determination of its affordability based on its value. In contrast, your internal customers – from middle management all the way through executive management and the shareholders – will pay great attention to your cost and price analysis. How much will you have to spend to develop the new features, and how much will you be able to charge for them at the end of the day? They will focus very much on the business financial analysis that we discussed in the section on *Financial Accounting*.

Although financial Return on Investment (RoI) will be key, the RoI is the end – not the beginning. The beginning is the qualitative value proposition. Let's begin with an apparently easy, but deceptively difficult, exercise – how would you qualify the value of your reading a book on business management in the context of increasing your personal value proposition?

If you've never thought about things in that context then think for a minute about what your current value proposition is. Can you articulate – for your direct supervisor – why you deserve the salary you receive? If you can do this well, you may plant the seed – why aren't you paid even more?

That may be an easy exercise, or it may be difficult – we all tend to think we are "entitled" to our salary, and rarely step back to ask if we are really earning it. So let's look at it from a different, more distanced, perspective. How would you articulate the value proposition for your favorite product?

As we just saw, part of each product life cycle is the technical aspect. A description of the work to be accomplished, and the schedule it will require, before the additional sales can be generated, and the return on investment can begin to be received.

A very simplistic, notional, business case is shown in Figure 17. As it shows, a business case – in its simplistic terms – is a promise that says "if you give me this much money, then I will generate this much in additional sales".

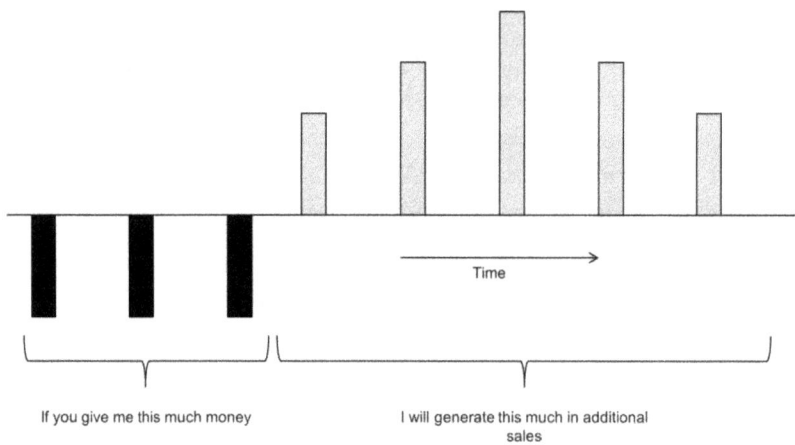

Figure 17. A Qualitative Business Case – Showing Investment and Return on Investment.

As we said earlier a business case is related to, but separate from, the value proposition. A great value proposition has a unique feature that only you can provide, and it is important to the person making the decision. A good value proposition qualifies the return on investment, the business case quantifies it.

The business case should also answer the question – how will the value proposition change?

- Will it add new features that will make your product more valuable to existing users?

- Will it add new features that will make your product appeal to more users?

- Will it address new requirements that will be needed for your product to compete?

- How much investment will be required to bring the idea to completion?

- Does the estimate include only "proof of concept" costs or also the costs to meet regulatory approvals, etc.?

- How "firm" is the budget estimate?

- Has it been formally reviewed and compared against past actual expenses, is it a ROM estimate, or …?

- How much in additional sales will be generated once the product is ready?

This last point is important. Do not include sales that will happen without the added features. Although there may be strategic or tactical reasons for endorsing one project over another, often it comes down to a simple financial comparison. The most fundamental choice is – should we invest the money, or return it to the shareholders as a dividend? If we choose to invest it, how should we invest it? In your project or in a savings account at the local bank? The basic choice is between risk and reward.

A given amount of money should have a different buying power today than it may in the future. The future value of money would account for the interest that would be earned over a given period of time. It may also account for inflation. Let's define a few terms.

Future Value (FV)

What an amount of money available today would be worth in the future. $100 invested today, in a bank account paying 3% yearly interest, would be worth $103 in one year's time. The FV of $100 today is $103 in one year.

Present Value (PV)

What an amount of money available in the future would be worth today. $97.09 invested today, in a bank account paying 3% yearly interest, would be worth $100 in one year's time. The PV of $100 a year from now is $97.09.

The mathematical relation between *FV* and *PV* is

$$FV = PV(1 + i)^n,$$

where

FV = Future Value

PV = Present Value

i = interest rate

n = # of years

Two other important terms are

Net Present Value (NPV)

Sum of the individual (yearly) PV of the cash flows.

Return on Investment (ROI)

Value of the return, less the cost of the investment.

A more specific business case is shown in Figure 18. In this example, specific quantifiable investments are examined against specific quantifiable returns. Would you invest your money in this project if your alternative was to put the money in a bank account that paid 3% yearly interest as described in Table 29?

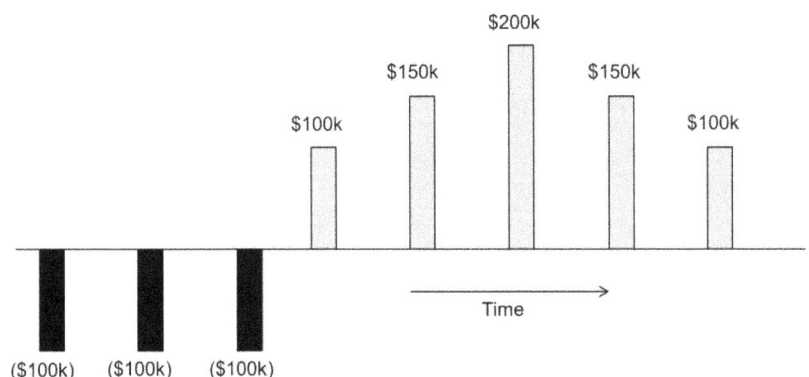

Figure 18. A Quantitative Business Case.

Table 29. Example RoI and NPV.

Interest Rate	3%							
	Year 1	Year 2	Year 3	Year 4	Year 5	Year 6	Year 7	Year 8
Investment	$(100.00)	$(100.00)	$(100.00)					
Sales				$ 100.00	$ 150.00	$ 200.00	$ 150.00	$ 100.00
		Subtotal	$(300.00)				Subtotal	$ 700.00
						Return on Investment (RoI)		$ 400.00
PV	$(100.00)	$ (97.09)	$ (94.26)	$ 88.85	$ 129.39	$ 167.50	$ 121.96	$ 78.94
		Subtotal	$(291.35)				Subtotal	$ 586.64
						Net Present Value (NPV)		$ 295.29

As this analysis shows, if you can give me $100 a year for three years – a total investment of $300 – then I will generate a $700 return in years 4 through 8. The difference is a return on investment of $700 – $300 = $400. But that $300 investment and $700 return are spread out of over 8 years. How much are they worth today?

The $100 I need you to give me today, to get me to the end of year 1, is worth $100. But at 3% interest, the $100 investment I need you to give me at the end of year 1, to get me to the end of year 2, could be generated from $97.09 invested in a banking account today. As the table shows, the $300 I need over three years could be generated from $291.35 invested today.

Likewise, that $100 return I give you at the end of year 8 could be generated from $78.94 invested in a banking account today. (That's a subtly, but we assume that we must supply the investment at the start of the year, and we don't generate the return until the end of the year.) That $700 total in year 8 is worth $586.64 today. Adding all those individual PVs up gives the NPV, which is $586.64 − $291.35 = $295.95. The NPV is positive − that's a good first step. But how good a ROI is that?

If I put the starting investment of $291.35 in a bank account today that pays 3% interest, we saw that in 3 years it would be worth $300. If we just leave it there, in 8 years it will be worth $358.32. What is the effective interest rate that turns that same investment of $291.35 into a value of $586.64 in 8 years? Calculating this interest rate is usually done by "trial and error". The solution to the example shown in Table 29, is given in Table 30. In this case, the Rate of Return (ROR) is 10.5%, which is more than the interest rate of 3% available from the bank, so we could conclude that this would be a good investment.

Let's give another, perhaps overly simplistic, example. Let's say that your friend has an idea for a professional development course that he believes could be sponsored by a large technical society dedicated to your industry. A ROM estimate is that it will take him, and a colleague, a total of 100 hours of time to develop the presentation material. They will both have to purchase plane tickets, a rental car, and hotel rooms to deliver the course. The technical society that sponsors the course will pay a total of $1000 / day, for two days, and provide free admission to a conference that is being held in conjunction with the course. The investment is notionally described in Figure 19. Is developing that course a good use of their time?

Table 30. Rate of Return.

Interest Rate	3%							
	Year 1	Year 2	Year 3	Year 4	Year 5	Year 6	Year 7	Year 8
Investment	$(100.00)	$(100.00)	$(100.00)					
Sales				$ 100.00	$ 150.00	$ 200.00	$ 150.00	$ 100.00
		Subtotal	$(300.00)				Subtotal	$ 700.00
						Return on Investment (RoI)		$ 400.00
PV	$(100.00)	$ (97.09)	$ (94.26)	$ 88.85	$ 129.39	$ 167.50	$ 121.96	$ 78.94
		Subtotal	$(291.35)				Subtotal	$ 586.64
						Net Present Value (NPV)		$ 295.29
Rate of Return	3.0%							
Year 1 Input	$ 100.00	$ 103.00	$ 106.09	$ 109.27	$ 112.55	$ 115.93	$ 119.41	$ 122.99
Year 2 Input	$ 97.09	$ 100.00	$ 103.00	$ 106.09	$ 109.28	$ 112.55	$ 115.93	$ 119.41
Year 3 Input	$ 94.26	$ 97.09	$ 100.00	$ 103.00	$ 106.09	$ 109.27	$ 112.55	$ 115.93
							Subtotal	$ 358.32
Rate of Return	0.192%							
Year 1 Input	$ 100.00	$ 100.19	$ 100.38	$ 100.58	$ 100.77	$ 100.96	$ 101.16	$ 101.35
Year 2 Input	$ 97.09	$ 97.28	$ 97.46	$ 97.65	$ 97.84	$ 98.03	$ 98.21	$ 98.40
Year 3 Input	$ 94.26	$ 94.44	$ 94.62	$ 94.80	$ 94.99	$ 95.17	$ 95.35	$ 95.53
							Subtotal	$ 295.29

Let's assume that the airline and hotel cost $500. Subtracting that expense from the gross income of $2,000 would leave a net income of $1500. Since you invested 100 hours to develop the course, and 32 hours to teach it, their hourly return on investment would be $1500 / 132 hrs = $11.36 / hr. This is just above the 2018 minimum wage of $11.00 / hr for the State of California, so we could conclude that it's not that good a ROI, in comparison to other things they could do with their time.

Purely from a cost perspective that might not make sense. However, there are some additional factors that might influence that decision, such as:

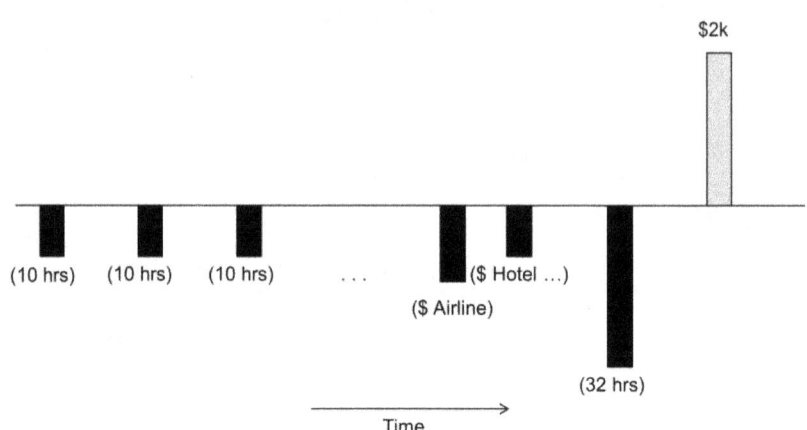

Figure 19. Example Cash Flow.

- Would you be able to teach that class more than once? The second time you wouldn't have to invest the initial 100 hours it took to develop the course, so your return would go up.

- Would teaching for the professional development society help give you visibility as an "expert" in your field?

- Would that visibility increase your value proposition in the eyes of your employer, and indirectly get you a bigger raise to keep you from being lured away to work for another company?

Our point is that not always does a business case come down to a simple financial comparison of alternatives, although that's often the starting point. Other factors might be tactical or strategic in nature, such as:

- Will the project increase our chances of winning a major pursuit?

- Will the project benefit a product line that is critical to future business?

Remember that plans sometimes fail because we "tunnel" and focus on "ideal" rather than "realistic". In other words, we neglect sources of uncertainty outside the plan itself. The unexpected almost always pushes in a single direction – higher costs and a longer time to completion. After all, how often have you left on trip and wound up getting there sooner than anticipated?

Having a solid business plan is a major accomplishment, but it's just one step in a longer process. You have to get the plan funded. You may be able to convince your company's internal management team to approve discretionary IR&D funding. Or you may deliver a proposal to an external customer, or venture capitalist, who can give you a contract to develop a new product. The details of how to do that will vary significantly from plan to plan, and from industry to industry. But once you get your project funded, you will need to monitor that project to ensure it successfully progresses from start to finish.

THE BUDGET ASPECT

A budget is a financial plan that is based on an estimate of expenses. In the business case we just looked at in Figure 18, we said we needed $100k a year. $100k would be the yearly budget. Although we all want to believe we're going to be wildly successful if we get our project approved, the reality is that not all projects succeed. One reason is that they go over budget.

To minimize the risk that they lose all of their investment, investors often insist on intermediate checkpoints. Maye they won't commit to giving you the full $300k for all three years right now, but they will give you $25k to get started and develop a more detailed plan.

If your business case depends on your being able to mature a critical technology to a higher TRL, the budget may clarify that you are only authorized up to a specific limit until you can demonstrate that the technology is ready. These check points give the investors' confidence that you're meeting your milestones and reducing the risk of failure.

The bottom line is that rather than just saying "I need $100k for next year", you will need to allocate those expenses to different tasks. Those individual budget allocations are how you will track progress. You may be under budget in some areas, and over budget in other areas, and still come in on target. In the section on Earned Value Management (EVM), we will look at specific tools you can use to measure how you are performing in comparison to both your budget, and schedule.

PROGRAM MANAGEMENT

Once we get a project approved, we have to successfully manage it to completion. Project management, or the equivalent term (to us) program management, is a key portion of every system as shown in Figure 20 and Figure 21. In the pages that follow, we aren't going to make any formal distinction between a project and a program. The terms are almost interchangeable, though we tend to think of projects as the smaller parts of larger programs.

In the discussion that follows we use the terminology recommended by the Project Management Institute (PMI), an internationally recognized not-for-profit professional association for the "project, program, and portfolio management profession".

The PMI offers certification as a Project Management Professional (PMP)™ and also publishes a standard reference *A Guide to the Project Management Body of Knowledge (PMBOK)*. Earlier versions of the PMBOK were recognized as standards by American National Standards Institute (ANSI), ANSI/PMI 99-001-2008, and Institute of Electrical and Electronics Engineers, IEEE 1490-2011.

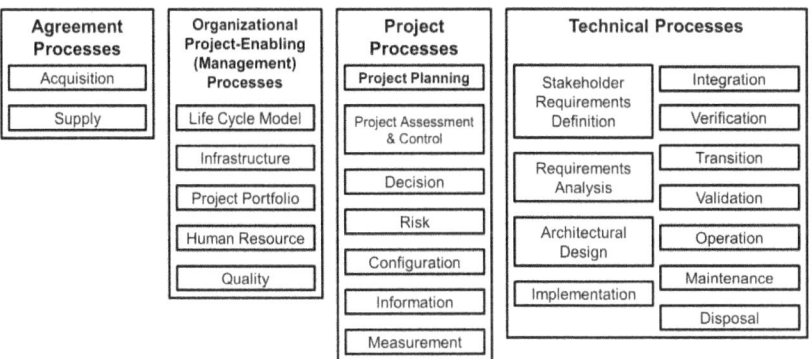

Figure 20. Systems and Software Engineering, System Life Cycle Processes, from IEEE Std 15288-2008.

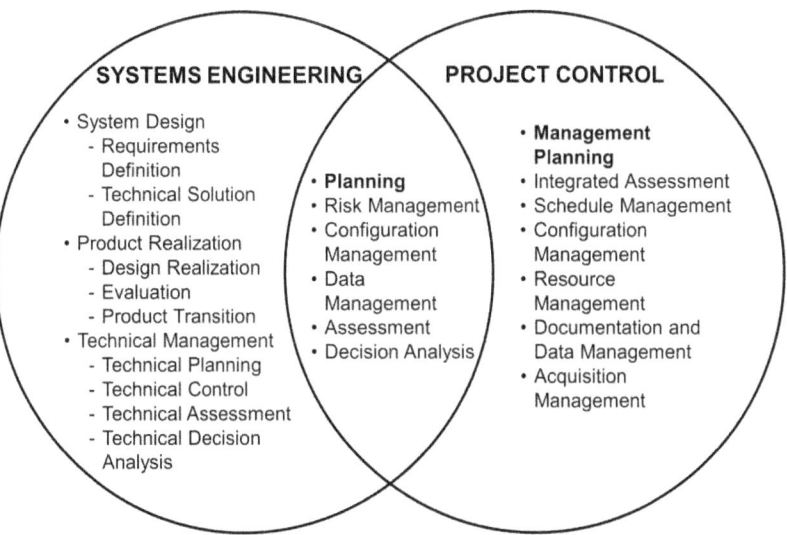

Figure 21. Systems Engineering and Project Control, from NASA Systems Engineering Hdbk, SP-2007-6105, Rev 1.

The PMBOK defines five process groups as shown in Table 31. The process groups look deceptively like life cycle phases, but as the PMBOK emphasizes, it is possible – and likely – to address each process group within a single life cycle phase. For example, the first step in most projects is getting approval – either making the business case or writing the proposal that gets you the okay to success. If you were seeking to write a proposal in response to a customer's RFP your first step would be "initiating". You would make a formal request of the approving authority for permission to develop a proposal.

Table 31. The Five Process Groups.

Process Groups	Definition
Initiating	Making the business case and getting approval
Planning	Making sure you are ready to begin
Executing	Doing it
Monitoring and Controlling	Making sure are doing it right
Closing	Transitioning to the next phase or the next project

Once approval is granted, you move into the "planning" phase. Here you would develop the high-level information you need to give to the proposal team to help them start writing the proposal.

Once the proposal planning is complete, you move into the "executing" phase – you begin to write the proposal. You then "monitor and control" the proposal development process, ensuring that you are making progress toward having a complete proposal in time to meet the deadline for proposal submission. Once the proposal is in, you move into "closing" the proposal effort. Keeping track of any remaining actions that need to be re-examined in a few weeks, or months, would be done during the "closing" process. Finally, after the proposal has been accepted and awarded, the same five process groups would be addressed again as you begin work on the program.

In addition to the process groups are the ten knowledge areas shown in Table 32. The first nine are the things that must be proactively managed during a project. The last one, integration, is an acknowledgement of the fact that the first nine need to be integrated together. The same Work Breakdown Structure you use to define "scope", is also used in the schedule that is used to monitor "time", and the budget that is used to monitor "cost", and so on. As that brief discussion implies, there are a number of artifacts that are generated in the course of initiating, planning, executing, monitoring and controlling, and closing a project. These are summarized in Table 33. In our opinion, much of being an effective program manager boils down to understanding the contents of this table.

As we mentioned, there are a multitude of courses available to assist you in preparing for PMI certification, so we won't bother doing a deep dive on these topics. However, we will do a brief pass through each of the knowledge areas to make sure we have a self-consistent understanding of what the knowledge area addresses, the artifacts that are used to help define it, and how the artifacts evolve as you step through the various process groups or life cycle phases.

Table 32. The Ten PMBOK Knowledge Areas.

Knowledge Areas	Definition
Scope	The work required, and only the work required, for completing the project successfully
Time	Schedule
Cost	Estimating, budgeting, financing, ...
Quality	Quality policies, objectives, and responsibilities
Human Resources	Acquisition, development, and management of the project team
Communications	The generation, collection, dissemination, storage, and ultimate disposition of project information
Risk	Identifying, analyzing, and responding to issues that can cause you to exceed technical, cost, or schedule metrics
Procurement	Purchasing or acquiring products, services, or results for the project
Stakeholder	Identifying and managing expectations
Integration	Identify, define, combine, unify and coordinate all other areas

Table 33. Key Project Management Artifacts.

	Planning	Monitoring & Controlling
Scope	• Statement of Work (SOW) • Technical Performance Measures (TPMs) • Work Breakdown Structure (WBS)	• Change Control Board (CCB)
Time	• Schedule	• Schedule Performance Indices (SPI) • To complete SPI (TSPI)
Cost	• Budget	• Cost Performance Indices (CPI) • To complete CPI (TCPI)
Quality	• Quality Requirements	• Acceptance Test Procedures (ATP) • Environmental Stress Screening (ESS) • Inspection
Human Resources	• Staffing Plan	• CPI, SPI, TCPI, TSPI
Communications	• Communications Plan	• Data Management
Risk	• Risk Register	• Risk Review Board (RRB)
Procurement	• Subcontracting Plan	• Subcontractor Deliveries
Stakeholder		• Situation Reports

Business Management for Engineers • 151

SCOPE

Scope is defined as:

The work required, and only the work required, for completing the project successfully.

Seems clear enough, but how will we know what is in scope for a project and what isn't? Quite simply, by documenting our assumptions. Artifacts that can help include: i) Statement of Work (SOW); and ii) Work Breakdown Structure (WBS). These are important, so let's spend a few minutes reviewing them.

Statement of Work (SOW)

As we saw earlier, a SOW may be a contractually binding document that specifies the scope of the effort you're being placed under contract to do. When part of a contract, it usually doesn't explicitly say what is not included, but for your internal company's planning purposes it never hurts to be explicit. After all, there's bound to be a re-organization or re-assignment of responsibilities sooner or later, and the next project manager won't be able to read your mind and will have to depend on how well you documented your scope statements.

On a huge program, like building a new aircraft, the complete SOW may be pages and pages in length. On a small Information Technology (IT) or Research & Development (R&D) project it may be just a couple of paragraphs.

Before jumping in and writing a SOW or scope statement we find it helpful to provide some structure in the form of a Work Breakdown Structure (WBS). Let's shift gears to the WBS and come back to the SOW later.

Work Breakdown Structure (WBS)

The (PMBOK) defines the WBS as a "deliverable oriented hierarchical decomposition of the work to be executed by the project team." What does that really mean? Fortunately, there are some standards out there that we could turn to for some crisp examples. The US MIL-HDBK-881C, Work Breakdown Structures for Defense Materiel Items, defines the WBS for an Aircraft System as shown in Table 34.

Table 34. Example Aircraft WBS from US MIL-STD-881C, (not all levels shown).

1	**Aircraft System**
1.1	Air Vehicle
1.1.1	Airframe
1.1.1.1	Airframe Integration, Assembly, Test and Checkout
1.1.1.2	Fuselage
1.1.1.3	Wing
1.1.1.4	Empennage
1.1.1.5	Nacelle
1.1.1.6	Other Aircraft Components 1 ... n (specify)
1.1.2	Propulsion
1.1.3	Vehicle Subsystems
1.1.4	Avionics
1.1.5	Armament / Weapons Delivery
1.1.6	Auxilliary Equipment
1.1.7	Furnishings and Equipment
1.1.8	Air Vehicle Software Release 1 ... n (specify)
1.1.9	Air Vehicle Integration, Assembly, Test and Checkout
1.2	System Engineering
1.3	Program Management
1.4	System Test and Evaluation
1.5	Training
1.6	Data
1.7	Peculiar Support Equipment
1.8	Common Support Equipment
1.9	Operational / Site Activation
1.10	Industrial Facilities
1.11	Initial Spares and Repair Parts

If you were planning on proposing a new aircraft for the US Military, you would be encouraged (or directed) to use this format as the starting point. Of course, we could continue to add additional levels of detail below that show, and we should do that as appropriate until we get down to a level appropriate for individual work packages. Work packages are formally defined in the section on *Earned Value Management*, but for now think of them as the lowest level building blocks of a program - pieces that a team of 2 – 3 people could complete in a month or less.

Once we have a framework to capture all of the effort, we are ready to more formally define the SOW. Just to be clear, the SOW and WBS usually are developed in parallel, and can be changed as required to make it clearer what you are going to do (or not do) and should be closely integrated.

Statement of Work (SOW), Continued

At the highest level, we probably need a crisp statement or two that describes exactly what we are doing so that we can explain it to upper management. Let's be clear, upper management doesn't need a shorter explanation because they're not as sharp as those of us in the engineering ranks. They need a shorter explanation because they farther removed from the project. They don't need to know – emphasis on <u>need</u> – the gory details to be able to understand what you're doing and how it fits into the rest of the business. If you've been entrusted to lead the project, you need to be crystal clear on what is in scope, and what is not, so you will be able to say "no – don't' do that" when it's appropriate, or "yes – continue" as required.

Let's start with a simplistic example and build up from there. Consider the following scope statement:

> The scope of this effort is limited to the labor costs associated with attendance at the program kick off meeting.

The kick off meeting will be attended by the Program Manager (PM), the Chief Engineer (CE), and the lead Systems Engineer (SE).

It is assumed that the kick off meeting will be three (3) full days in duration, and that each member of the travel team will require five (5) full days to prepare for the meeting, one half day to travel out to the meeting; one half day to travel back from the meeting; and three (3) full days to respond to action items after the meeting.

Is it clear what is in scope, and what is not in scope, from this statement? We think it's pretty clear. Here we've acknowledged that there are some labor costs associated with attending the kick of meeting. They are included in this element of the SOW.

At the same time, it's pretty clear that something important is not included in this element of the SOW – travel costs. This is a warning sign that we should confirm that those travel costs are included somewhere else. We should have a separate WBS element for travel such as:

The scope of this effort is limited to the travel costs, (e.g., airfare, rental car, hotel, meals, ...), associated with attending the program kick off meeting in Washington, DC.

The kick off meeting will be attended by the Program Manager (PM), the Chief Engineer (CE), and the lead Systems Engineer (SE).

It is assumed that the kick off meeting will be three (3) full days in duration, and that the travel team will require one-half day of travel out, and one-half day of travel back, in addition to a single rental car and hotel rooms.

Business Management for Engineers ▪ 155

Again, is it clear what is in scope, and what is not in scope, from this statement? As before, we think it's pretty clear. Here we've acknowledged that there are travel costs – in addition to labor costs. Travel is included in this element of the SOW. If we were reviewing the program plan we could confirm that there were both labor costs and travel costs required for the program kick off meeting, so there were no obvious gaps. (By the way, there's nothing wrong with including both travel costs and labor costs in the same WBS element, but we think it's cleaner to split travel and labor, so that's the method we follow.)

Now could an independent observer read those scope statements and confirm that they are absolutely correct? Probably not – they'd have to go confirm the meeting duration, number of attendees required, and so on. But they could easily confirm that the assumptions are self-consistent, (and when in doubt, be self-consistent even if you might not be right). Furthermore, they would probably be considered to be "reasonable" assumptions. If they seem unreasonable, then there's the start of a good conversation with the person or group providing the funding:

> "Why did you assume a three day kick off meeting?"
>
> "Because we've done six similar programs in the past two years, and the kick off meeting for each of those programs was three days long."

Regardless of whether you are right or not, you have an answer that you can defend. A casual observer can see what you're doing, and what you're not doing, and that's the start of understanding.

But of course, travel to kick off meetings is probably a very small part of a big project, such as "build a new airplane". How would we scale this answer up to a larger project?

For a larger project, you'd have a much broader scope statement at the highest level, something like

> To design, develop, build, test, and deliver three (3) prototype aircraft that meet the requirements specified in the SOW.

Let's do a quick comparison of this SOW with the tasks identified back in Table 34.

- Level 1.1 of the WBS addressed the Air Vehicle and all its subsystems. Looks like that's included in our scope statement.

- Level 1.2 of the WBS addressed System Engineering. We didn't mention it explicitly in the scope statement, but seems reasonable to assume that system engineering is in scope since their job will be to coordinate the design, development, build, ...

- Level 1.3 of the WBS addressed Program Management. As with System Engineering, we didn't mention it explicitly in the scope statement, but it seems reasonable to assume it is in scope.

- Level 1.4 of the WBS addressed System Test and Evaluation. The scope statement included "test", so this is definitely in scope.

- Level 1.5 of the WBS addressed Training. The scope statement didn't mention training, so this is probably not included. If it should be, there's a gap in our scope.

- Level 1.6 of the WBS addressed Data. The scope statement didn't mention data by name, but it's hard to design, develop, build or test anything without developing data. Is it included? Probably, but maybe we ought to clarify that either in the scope statement itself, or in the sections that follow.

- Level 1.7 of the WBS addressed peculiar support equipment. Again, the scope statement didn't mention support equipment by name. It's possible to design, develop, build or test an aircraft and not deliver the equipment required to support it once it's in the field. This looks like a gap.

That's enough of a review to get the idea. We need to make sure that the WBS and SOW are tied off – integrated – and that they clarify exactly what is in scope and make it possible to understand what is out of scope.

Monitoring and Controlling Scope

After we have planned our scope, and begun to execute it, the next step is to monitor and control it. How do we monitor, and control scope?

First, let's agree that monitoring and controlling scope is very important. If you don't do it properly you fall into one of the sure-fire ways to go over budget and fall behind schedule – scope creep. Scope creep is the term used to describe what happens when we allow the boundary between what is in scope and out of scope to become blurred and begin to take on work that we never committed to doing. As soon as this happens we spend more labor hours, and more schedule time, completing that next piece of code because we decided to add a few minor features that would really make it better code – more capable, more easily adaptable to future changes, and so on. There may be great "technical" reasons for desiring those changes, but if we didn't get formal approval to include those changes as part of our scope statement we shouldn't do them. If we do, we'll need more cost and more time than we planned on, so we find ourselves over budget and behind schedule.

How do we avoid scope creep? By monitoring and controlling scope proactively. We monitor scope by making sure we have a clear understanding of what we plan to accomplish – and what we don't plan to accomplish – before we authorize new work to begin. This could be as simple as monitoring how many people we send to the kick off meeting. We planned to send three people in our example. If we decide to send four people – because the customer wanted a test engineer present for some of the discussions – the addition of the test engineer to the travel team is scope creep. It wasn't in the original plan, so if we decide to do it we'll incur unexpected costs. That doesn't mean we can't do it – it just means we need to acknowledge that it wasn't in the plan if we do decide to do it. In other words, we agree to fund that additional person out of management reserve (defined in the section on *Earned Value Management*) or we agree that we'll have to cut one person from the travel team when we go to the six-month program review and make up the cost there. That is how we control scope. By making a conscious decision to do, or not, do something before we start.

Often controlling scope comes down to one simple word in the English language – No. We tell people no – don't add that other feature to the code; no – don't take the test engineer to the kick off meeting; no – don't repeat the entire acceptance test procedure, only repeat section three; and so on. Of course, sometimes we have to say yes. Okay – add the ability for the software to take in any real value between 0 and 100, not just integer values; Yes – take the test engineer to the kick off meeting, but only for the first two days; Yes – repeat Section three of the Acceptance Test Procedure, we want to make sure we didn't break anything in the software interface when we added that new feature; and so on.

The best way to control scope is via a formal Change Control Board (CCB) – a committee that has to formally approve any changes before they are made. Nobody takes on new scope unless it is approved, and a budget is assigned. The CCB members may include the program manager (the person ultimately responsible for cost and schedule), the chief engineer (the person ultimately responsible for meeting the technical requirements), test (the person ultimately responsible for making sure the widget meets the contractual requirements), as well as quality, finance, contracts, and so on.

TIME

Time in this context is virtually identical to schedule, and in fact the key artifact in time management is the schedule. The master program schedule lists all the activities required, and how they are related to one another. A notional example for a US DoD procurement is shown in Figure 22. The schedule should identify and define all required activities and should of course show the duration of the activities and the number and type of resources required (e.g., hardware engineers, software engineers, test engineers, …).

The sequence of project activities that add up to the longest overall duration – in other words the minimum amount of time it will take to complete all required activities – is known as the critical path. The critical path, as the name implies, identifies the "critical" activities that must be completed on time, or the completion date of the project will slip. Activities that are not on the critical path typically have some slack, or float, (the gap between their expected end date and the start date of the next task) and can be delayed without impacting the overall project completion date.

How do we monitor time (e.g., the schedule)? By comparing actual completion dates, to predicted completion dates. If we thought updating the software interface would take two weeks, and it's still not done after three weeks, we're behind schedule. Schedule Performance Indices (SPI), discussed in the *Earned Value Management (EVM)* section, is a helpful tool.

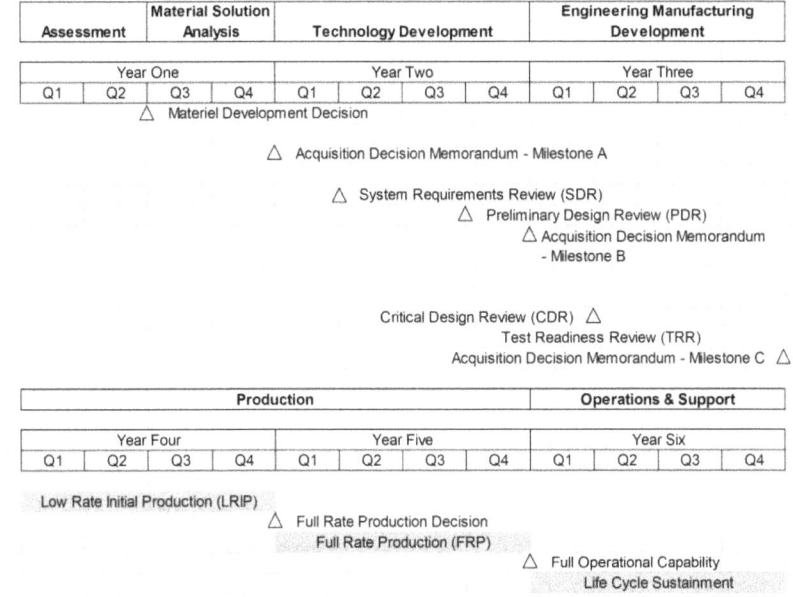

Figure 22. A Notional Schedule.

How do we control time (e.g., the schedule)? By assigning more resources – more personnel or equipment. If we're behind schedule, we could assign more people to help with finishing the work. Sounds simple to say that, but reality is not that crisp. How will the new people know what to do and how to do it? If the old people stop working and train them of course. So, we may very well fall further behind, before we begin to move ahead at a faster pace. This is one of the arts of program management – is it better to just leave the team alone until they figure it out, or do we really need to step in and assign more resources, or reassign people to other tasks where they can be more successful?

Where do we get the money to pay for the new people? We can either take it from management reserve – funding we set aside to pay for this type of unexpected, but in scope, activities; by cutting funding for another task – which may require changing its scope statement; or we have to accept that it's going to put us over budget.

COST

Cost in this context is virtually identical to budget, and in fact the key artifact in time management is the budget. We build up the budget from the cost of the individual work packages. If we don't like the final answer, because it's unaffordable, we have to look at different technical approaches, or changes to the scope, and see if one of them will make the cost more affordable.

The section on Earned Value Management (EVM) provides a comprehensive discussion of various financial metrics that can be used to monitor costs, such as Cost Performance Indices (CPI) and To complete Cost Performance Indices (TCPI). At the end of the day, we monitor costs by comparing the actual cost to complete a task, to the predicted cost to complete. If we thought updating the software interface would take $10,000, and it's still not done after we've spent $15,000, then we're over budget.

How do we control cost? Spending more money is easy. It's spending less money that's hard. Spending less money once you're over budget requires you to cut another part of the project or cover the overrun from management reserve. We wanted to add ten new features, but we only have enough money to add eight. In some cases, you can ease the requirements. If getting a 1% performance improvement out of the system requires 10% more cost, maybe getting to 99% of the performance goal is good enough.

Of course, there may be cheaper ways to get the work done than originally planned. Subcontracting, or outsourcing, the work to a company with lower costs who could perform the work more cheaply is a possibility. But that begs the question – if we knew they were a cheaper option, why didn't we plan on doing that from the start? Depending on your company's rate structure, it may be possible to use less expensive personnel than originally planned.

QUALITY

A simplistic definition of quality is "how good or bad something is". In a program management context, quality is better defined as "the degree to which a set of inherent characteristics fulfills requirements". Many requirements are functional in nature, they describe specific behaviors. The non-functional requirements can be thought of as the "quality attributes". These are often called the "ilities" like reliability, maintainability, stability, portability, testability, scalability, and so on.

Quality must be designed into a product. For a product to operate reliably 99.99% of the time, it places constraints on how seldom any element of the product could fail. This leads to design choices such as redundancy, and places constraints on materials and processes. An example of the different reliability relations that are applied to components connected in series or in parallel is shown in Figure 23.

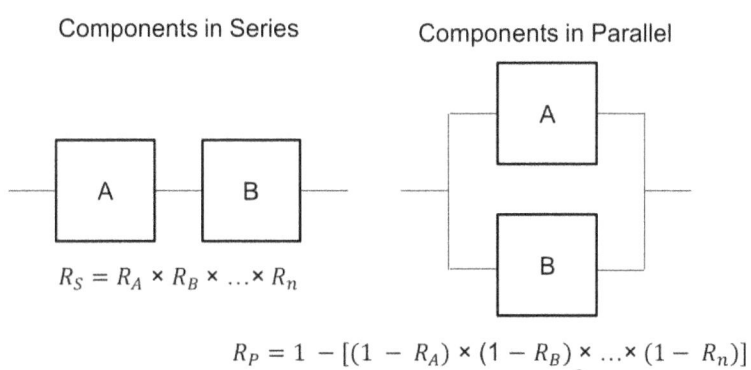

$$R_S = R_A \times R_B \times ... \times R_n$$

$$R_P = 1 - [(1 - R_A) \times (1 - R_B) \times ... \times (1 - R_n)]$$

Figure 23. Reliability Relation for Series and Parallel Components.

More generally, the field of quality control has evolved from Statistical Quality Control (SQC), to Statistical Process Control (SPC), to Total Quality Management (TQM), and Six Sigma. More recently terminology like lean manufacturing, lean production, or simply "lean" are used to describe any tools that can help eliminate waste in the production system.

A related term is Quality Assurance, which are the processes used to improve the production processes to minimize issues that could lead to quality defects. This may include workmanship standards, tied to work processes and assembly procedures, to ensure repeatability.

The key take away here is that quality must be managed, just like scope, time, and cost. There is probably a quality group in your company that understands the finer points of quality control and quality assurance. Bring them into the project early. As we stated earlier, quality must be designed in. It's a lot easier to do it correctly at the start, rather than try and add it in later.

HUMAN RESOURCES

Human resources refer to the people who will be part of the project team. Like scope, time, cost, and quality, the staffing needs of the project need to be planned and managed. Managing Human Resources refer to the processes involved in the planning, acquisition, development, and management of the project team. On smaller projects, this may be trivial. "I need half of Bob's time for four weeks." On major projects, this can be daunting. We could have a need for dozens, or hundreds, of engineers with varying skill sets. How would we know if they will be available once the project gets the go ahead? Will we need to hire new staff? Will we need to train old ones to have new skills? Better to think about all of this up front, during the proposal stages, rather than wait until the contract has been awarded and realize you can't execute the program.

The staffing plan often flows from the schedule. The schedule assumes a given amount of work is accomplished within a specific amount of time, and that equates to a specific number of engineers with the right skills to do the work. Looking at the schedule it should be easy to estimate the "demand". How many staff members are required to meet the demands of the schedule? Do they account for the expected turnover rate, due to retirements or people who may leave to seek other employment? If they're not available in my department, could they be loaned in from other departments?

Compare the demand to the supply. How many engineers, with the right skill sets, are currently employed – and expected to be available to work on this project? Having a staffing level of 10,000 engineers doesn't help much, if the organization already has enough work to do to keep 12,000 engineers busy before your project gets added in the mix.

If employees aren't available internally, should we look at permanent hires? These are of course people who will become full-time employees, and many of them would be expected to remain employees until they retire. Or should we look at temporary hires? Hire people from a job shop house with the right skills that would contribute to the project for a few weeks, or months, but would not be expected to become full-time employees? Either option may be viable given the specific needs of you project.

Once we get the right people and they begin to work, how do we monitor progress to confirm that we have the right staffing level in place? Often the same metrics that measure cost and schedule, CPI and SPI, are sufficient. They confirm if the right number of hours are being charged to the project to keep it on schedule. If not, they help highlight the areas of the project that are under staffed, or over staffed.

RISK (AND OPPORTUNITY)

The dictionary defines risk as the possibility that something bad or unpleasant will happen. Similarly, an opportunity is the possibility that something good or pleasant will happen. In a project management context, risks are things that could cause you to miss a technical, cost, or schedule performance metric. That is, risks are things that could cause you to fall short of a technical requirement, go over budget, or fall behind schedule. Similarly, opportunities are things that could cause you to exceed a technical requirement, come in under budget, or ahead of schedule.

Risk, and opportunity, management is the process involved with identifying, analyzing, and controlling the risks, and opportunities, for the project. The first step is of course to identify the risks. What are the myriad of things that could, if they occur, cause bad things to happen.

A technical risk might be

- We may not be able to optimize the algorithm so that it generates an answer in 0.1 msec

A cost risk might be

- We may not be able get fit the algorithm within the low cost Field Programmable Gate Array (FPGA) planned

A schedule risk might be

- The vendor may be late in delivering the FPGA

Of course, identifying the risks is only first step toward managing them. You then have to analyze what the impact of the risk would be. This analysis could be either qualitative or quantitative. We prefer an "If ..., then ..." format. For example,

Technical

- If we cannot get the algorithm to complete processing in 0.1 msec, then we will have to move the function to an Application Specific Integrated Circuit (ASIC).

Cost

- If we cannot fit the algorithm in the low cost FPGA, then we will have to buy a larger FPGA which is more expensive.

Schedule

- If the vendor is late in delivering the FPGA, then integration will be delayed.

Once the risks are identified, the next step in analysis is to determine how likely the risk is to happen? What is the impact to the technical, cost, or schedule metric? How likely is the risk to become realized? What can we do now, to minimize the probability of occurrence or have a fall back plan ready if the original approach doesn't work as planned?

Risks are often documented in a risk register. A matrix that lists information such as:

- Risk
- Category (technical, cost, schedule)
- Probability of the risk occurring
- Impact of the risk if it occurs
- Actions to mitigate the risk, ...

An example risk register is shown below in Table 35.

Used properly, the risk register can help the project team understand what additional actions are required. In some cases, we will choose to mitigate the risks, perhaps by funding development of two parallel designs, and then do a down select. In other cases, we may order similar components from two different vendors and down select later based on quality, cost, etc. Still other times, we simply accept the risk. The probability of it occurring, or the cost to mitigate it, do not justify the expense.

#	Description	Category	Probability	Cost Impact	Schedule Impact
1	If we cannot get the algorithm to complete processing in 0.1 msec, then we will have to move the function to an Application Specific Integrated Circuit (ASIC).	Technical	10%	$1M	6 months
2	If we cannot fit the algorithm in the low cost FPGA, then we will have to buy a larger FPGA which is more expensive	Cost	25%	$250k	2 weeks
3	If the vendor is late in delivering the FPGA, then integration will be delayed	Schedule	15%	$0	Day for Day

Table 35. Example Risk Register.

For additional information on risk, see:

- ISO/IEC Guide 73:2009 (2009). Risk management — Vocabulary. International Organization for Standardization.

- ISO/DIS 31000 (2009). Risk management — Principles and guidelines on implementation. International Organization for Standardization.

COMMUNICATIONS

Communications – the flow of information between stakeholders – should also be managed.

Communication management refers to the processes involved in ensuring timely and appropriate generation, collection, dissemination, storage, and ultimate disposition of project information

What information needs to flow out of the project? To whom? How frequently? In what format? Who has responsibility for providing the information? Some of the information required may be formal program deliverables. A monthly status report that summarizes progress toward technical, cost, and schedule goals – and also discusses risks or issues that may cause problems in the near future.

Equally important is the informal flow of information. If the program manager of the sponsoring agency has a question, do they call your program manager – and only your program manager – or can they pick up the phone and call the engineer actually doing the work? If they can call your engineer, can they call your subcontractor?

Although engineers may be very familiar with the technical details of the work, they are not always insightful as to the repercussions of issues that may arise. They may make an off handed remark like – the subcontractor sent the wrong parts, so we're behind schedule – and not think through the implications of what being behind schedule could mean to the customer. Having a more formal customer contact plan – that clarifies who on the project talks to who on the customer side – can minimize the possibility of sending mixed messages and gives the project management team time to fully think through the implications of the message before its delivered.

Don't misunderstand, we are not suggesting that it's okay to mislead the customer. But there's a difference between not delivering bad information until you can confirm how bad it is and explain the work around plan and choosing not to deliver bad information at all. Especially if you know it's bound to be discovered at some point anyway. Don't mislead the customer, but at the same time, think through the message so the customer can get an understanding that you're actively working the problem.

Also, as we'll see in the Section on Communicating with Executive Leadership, the content of a message that should flow to the program manager is necessarily different from the type of information you would share with your engineering colleagues.

Part of managing communications may be appointing a formal data manager – the person who submits all contract deliverables to the customer. They provide a crisp log of what got delivered and when, so there's a record in case anybody asks for a copy of something they thought got delivered six months ago but couldn't find.

On larger programs, you may want to formally require approval of all messages, speakers, etc. These are the people who are formally recognized as speaking for the company. If a major program is behind schedule or over cost, the company stock price may suffer so you will want to control who delivers that message.

PROCUREMENT

Procurement refers to the processes involved with purchasing or acquiring products, services, or results for the project. Are we going to use approved vendors, so we don't have to worry about the possibility of a low-cost bidder providing counterfeit parts? Do we have a strategic sourcing agreement with a vendor that guarantees them an opportunity to bid on our part needs before any other vendors are asked to submit a quote? Do we just need a handful of parts for a proof of concept prototype that will remain with the engineering group in perpetuity, or will we need thousands of parts to go into production units that will become the property of the customer?

Who can help with all of that? The subcontracts manager. Remember, subcontracts gives to your subcontractors, contracts receives from your customer.

STAKEHOLDERS

Finally, we want to manage the processes involved in keeping the stakeholders informed about our progress. This is something that will likely be heavily tailored to each individual project, but it starts with answering questions like:

- Who are the key stakeholders that need to, or want to, be informed about how the project is progressing?

- What level of influence do they have over the project, or future projects?

- What information do they want to see?

- What format do they want it in? (e.g., an informal email on Friday afternoon, or a formal briefing every other Tuesday)

The rule of thumb is simply that the more power the stakeholder has over the project, and the more interested they are in monitoring it, the more closely you will want to proactively manage them.

INTEGRATION

One of the characteristics of a good project plan is that all the program artifacts are in agreement and traceable (self-consistent). They must all be integrated. If you come up with a WBS structure to capture the different elements of the SOW, use the same WBS headings in the schedule, and for the work packages you use in compiling the budget.

A good program plan is also realistic. It takes one woman nine months to have a baby, but that doesn't mean that nine women can't have a baby in one month. The program plan, when successfully executed, allows you to fulfill the promises in your business case. It's important to appreciate that going over budget during development rapidly erodes your business case. If you realize that you need an additional $1M investment, to offset that additional cost you would need to generate an additional $10M in sales, at 10% profit margin, just to break even. Being late to market can be just as bad as going over budget, because it gives the competition time to catch up or pass you.

BUSINESS DEVELOPMENT

Rumor has it, if you build a better mousetrap the world will beat a path to your door. But how will the world know if you build a better mousetrap? Once they do find out, will the path to your door be sufficiently wide, straight, sturdy, ... to withstand all that traffic?

The Business Development organization is there to help answer those kinds of questions. It's important to start thinking about how to sell your product or service sooner, rather than later. Basic questions like:

- What are you trying to sell?
- How will you sell it?
- Who will want to buy it?
- Why will they want to buy it?

And equally important, but longer-term questions like:

- How long will you be able to continue to sell your product
    - Without adding new features?
    - Before the competition offers a lower cost version?

SALES

The sales team is responsible for understanding the customers' business, on an individual basis. Externally, they are the voice of your company to the customer. Their job is to educate the customer on how your products and services can help solve their problems. Internally, they are the voice of the customer. They speak for the customer when the customer is not in the room.

The sales team seeks to understand the problem the customer is trying to solve. They then educate the customer on your products by giving briefings, gauging the response, and suggesting "Did you know that we have a solution available now?"

The sales team's responsibility is for near term Pursuit and Order Capture (POC). Their job is to close the sale. To bring back an order so that engineering will have something to design or manufacturing will have something to build. In short, the sales team tries to fill the sales funnel. What's the sales funnel you ask? Let's explain.

In most organizations there's a strong desire for long term growth. They want a positive slope to the projected revenue curve, but typically cannot completely identify the specific business deals they plan on winning. That leaves a gap, roughly in the shape of a funnel, as shown in Figure 24. The sales team is there to convert near term prospects into sales.

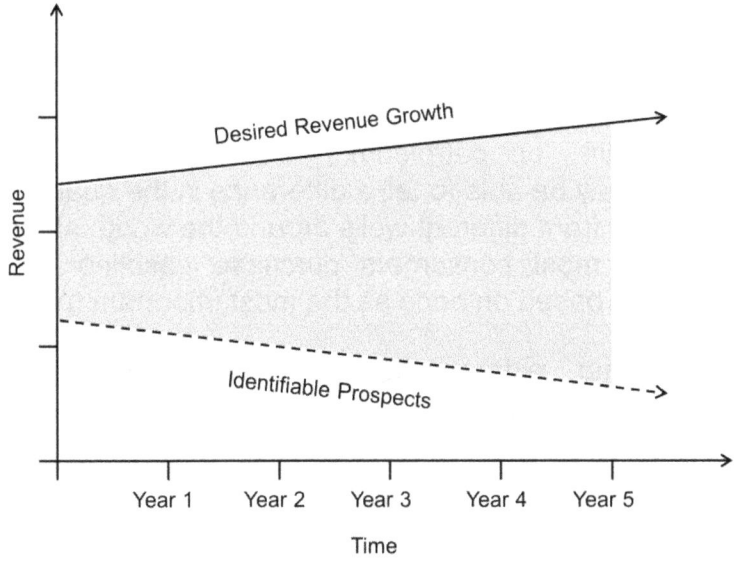

Figure 24. The Sales Funnel.

The sales team also helps define the pursuit strategy for proposals. What do we need to do now, to make sure they buy our product next year? Part of their job is also to forecast future business. How many units might we sell next year or the year after, and to whom?

How can you tell when the sales team is doing their job well? If you are winning your fair share of new business opportunities. An effective sales team increases the probability of winning. Without an effective sales team, business drops off and staffing cuts are sure to follow.

First, let's define a couple of terms. Economists speak of products in terms of differentiation – literally how different a product is perceived to be relative to competing products. On the low end of the differentiation scale are commodities, which are defined as

> a good or service whose wide availability typically leads to smaller profit margins and diminishes the importance of factors (such as brand name) other than price

Commodities are things we tend to buy primarily based on price. This includes a lot of raw materials like precious metals, grain, or petroleum. Although the chemical engineers may be able to tell a difference in the quality of the oil produced from different wells around the world, at the end of the day most consumers purchase gasoline for their automobiles based on price as the most important factor.

At the other extreme are products that are easily differentiated from the competition based on factors such as:

- Functionality
- Quality
- Availability

One of the jobs the sales team does is to try and create differentiation between the competition. If they can convince the buyer that there really is a difference, and that difference is worth paying more for, then they have successfully done their job. This requires a good understanding of why the customer is buying the product in the first place.

Obviously, you wouldn't try to sell a satellite launch vehicle to a company that builds airplanes, you would sell it to a company that builds spacecraft. So, finding the right buyer is the first step. Also, the customers who buy new aircraft are probably different from the customers who buy engines for new aircraft. In the first case, airlines buy new aircraft. In the second case, aircraft manufacturers buy new engines. This illustrates a bit of the hierarchy in the industry.

At the higher level are the Original Equipment Manufacturers (OEMs). These are the companies that provide the completed systems – the new aircraft or spacecraft. Beneath them are the first-tier suppliers that sell completed subsystems, such as avionics or engines, directly to the OEMs. Beneath them are the second-tier suppliers that sell components, such as machined parts or FPGAs, directly to the first-tier suppliers. Understanding who buys your product, and why they buy is, is the job of the sales team.

No one in the organization, other than your direct chain of command, has more influence on your product line or career than sales. If they can't sell it, you can't get paid to design or build it.

MARKETING

The marketing team is responsible for understanding how the entire customer base (the market) will evolve in the near term. That is, they try to understand where the customer base that forms your addressable market plans to go in the next few years, as well as the market forces that could accelerate or decelerate those plans.

Externally, the marketing team tries to shape future requirements to favor your products. Internally, they try to shape product line roadmaps to meet future (emerging) requirements. They are the ones that try to bridge the gap between what you are selling today and what customers may want to buy tomorrow.

How do they do this? With the help of the sales team, they develop an understanding of how the entire market is changing. Are they hearing a consistent theme from all of their major customers? If so, that's a good sign that the market is changing in that direction.

Once they have that information they try to educate your company's product line managers on how their products should evolve to meet emerging needs. Everybody is asking for ____. What's our plan to give it to them? The competition is telling our customers they'll be ready in three years. Can we be ready in two?

We think of marketing as shown in Figure 25. In this example, the customers are asking for something you don't sell – a spoon. Nobody wants to buy what you do sell – forks. What do you do? You can either get out of the fork business and into the spoon business or try and bridge the gap by meeting in the middle – a spork. You can do this if you can convince the customer that a spork can do everything a spoon can do, almost, plus it allows you to pick up food with the pointy part at the end.

Marketing's responsibility is for far term pursuit and order capture. If you don't know where the market is going, you won't have time to be first to market. They try to position the company for future success, typically just 3 – 5 years into the future. They also influence the pursuit strategy and help forecast future business.

Figure 25. A Simple Marketing Example.

STRATEGY

The strategy team is responsible for positioning the business for long term growth. Externally, they try to understand how the business models that are working in the market today may need to change. Internally, they try to position the company for the best competitive advantage in the long term. Their focus is on the business model - the plan for how you will make money. The business model includes things like

- An explanation of the products and services you will provide
- A plan for how you will manufacture / provide them
- An understanding of the expenses you will incur in providing them

- A description of the specific market you are targeting
- An estimate of the revenue you will generate

How does the strategy team do this? They make sure they understand today's business model and look for signs that will help them understand how the business model may change in the future. Make no mistake, your business model will change. Digital cameras brought about the end of most film cameras. The internet changed purchasing habits of consumers.

In the book *Collapse: How Societies Choose to Fail or Succeed*, Jared Diamond examined many of the civilizations who thrived at one point in the past couple of thousand years, only to shrink to irrelevance in 2 or 3 generations. He found that one trait that all had in common was that they failed to appreciate that what "got them great" in the first place, was not sufficient to "keep them great" in the long term. This is strategy's job – to understand when it's time to cut the ties to what got you great and strike out in new directions that may be necessary to keep you great.

They position the company for the best competitive advantage in the long term by asking if "radical" changes are required. How much longer will this market be profitable? What can we do to make it more profitable? When should we consider exiting the market?

They also influence mergers and acquisitions, and discretionary spending. Should we buy a competitor in order to stay viable? Why should we continue to invest in a dying product line?

If you don't have a plan for how your business will continue to grow, investors will take their money elsewhere. Strategy focuses on analyzing market needs and anticipates how our business model may need to change.

CHAPTER 7
EVALUATING SUCCESS

Even if we come up with a great idea, successfully bringing that idea to life in the market place takes work. It takes time to ensure that the concept is sound technically, and financially viable, as you define a business model, strategy for taking it to market, market analysis to size the business opportunity, prep the sales team on how to differentiate it from the competition, and ultimately complete the design, manufacturing, and test to make the product a reality. Even if we do all of those things right, the product can flop in the market place. So how are we to judge whether a project – or business – is successful?

In this chapter we'll look at a variety of tools used to gauge financial success. We'll begin by explaining how to develop a business case for a new concept. We will then show how a process called Earned Value Management (EVM) can be used to monitor the progress of a development program. Finally, we look at some tools used to measure the success of a portfolio, business unit, and corporation.

PROJECT SUCCESS – EARNED VALUE MANAGEMENT

The art or science of project management is to find a way to achieve the project goals, while honoring the budget and schedule constraints. A standard approach for monitoring cost and schedule that is used on US defense programs is Earned Value Management (EVM). This approach is recommended by the US Defense Acquisition University (DAU) and is listed in the FAR as Subpart 243.2. Quoting from Subpart 234.201, the DoD applies the earned value management system requirement as follows:

- For cost or incentive contracts and subcontracts valued at $20,000,000 or more, the earned value management system shall comply with the guidelines in the American National Standards Institute/Electronic Industries Alliance Standard 748, Earned Value Management Systems (ANSI/EIA-748)

- For cost or incentive contracts and subcontracts valued at $50,000,000 or more, the contractor shall have an earned value management system that has been determined by the cognizant Federal agency to be in compliance with the guidelines in ANSI/EIA-748

The basic concept behind EVM is that focusing on cost or schedule alone can be misleading. We must look at cost and schedule in relation to the work required. For example, if we are six months into a yearlong project and have spent half of the money allocated for the entire project, are we on budget? Not if we have only accomplished 30% of the work and had 70% of the work to go. In this case, we're behind schedule and the project is likely to come in over budget. Similarly, if we spent half the money and got half the work done but were eight months into a yearlong project then we're on budget, but behind schedule. Let's introduce three complementary, but distinct, terms:

Budgeted Cost of Work Scheduled (BCWS)

> The cost you budgeted for the work you had scheduled up through a specific point in the time.

Budgeted Cost of Work Performed (BCWP)

> The cost you budgeted for the work that was actually performed through a specific point in time.

Actual Cost of Work Performed (ACWP)

> The actual cost the work that was actually performed through a specific point in time.

Consider a simplistic example of a project that planned to accomplish work at a linear rate as shown in Figure 26.[11] The BCWS for the work scheduled through today is shown, and the total budget for the entire project, at completion, is known simply as the Budget at Completion (BAC).

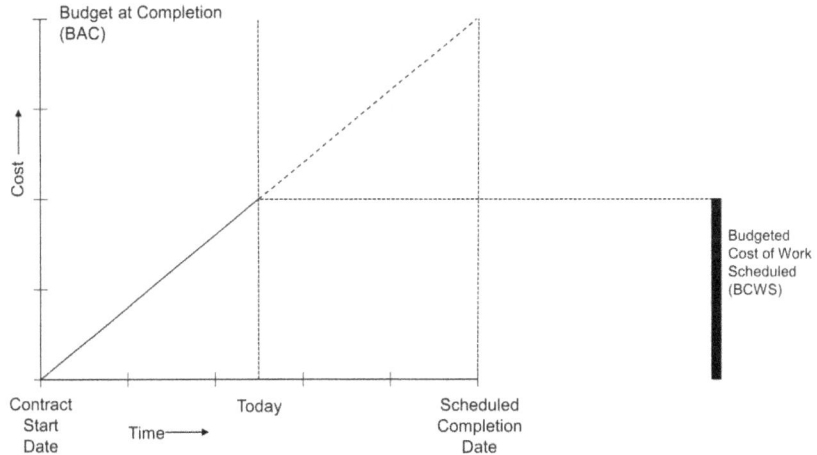

Figure 26. Cost vs Time for a Project with a Linear Work Rate.

What if the project is incurring cost at a rate below that planned as shown in Figure 27. At this point in time actual costs are less than budgeted costs. Will the project come in under budget and on schedule? We won't know unless we also look at the amount of work actually completed.

If work is being completed at an even lower rate, Figure 28, then clearly, we have accomplished less work than planned and are behind schedule. Even though costs are tracking below what was planned, we are still over budget because we paid more than planned for the work that was actually completed. Figure 28 indicates a program that is both behind schedule and over budget because we are not getting the value planned for the money spent.

---

[11] Some of the figures that follow can be hard to visualize in black and white, so a color version is available at the book's web site.

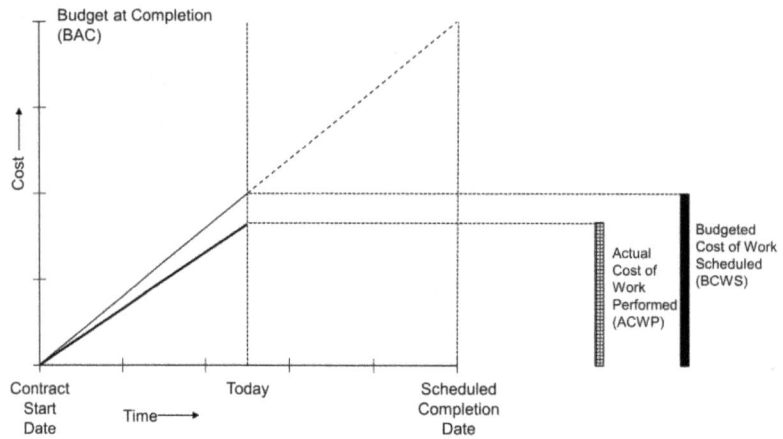

Figure 27. Actual Cost Growing at a Rate Below That of the Work Scheduled.

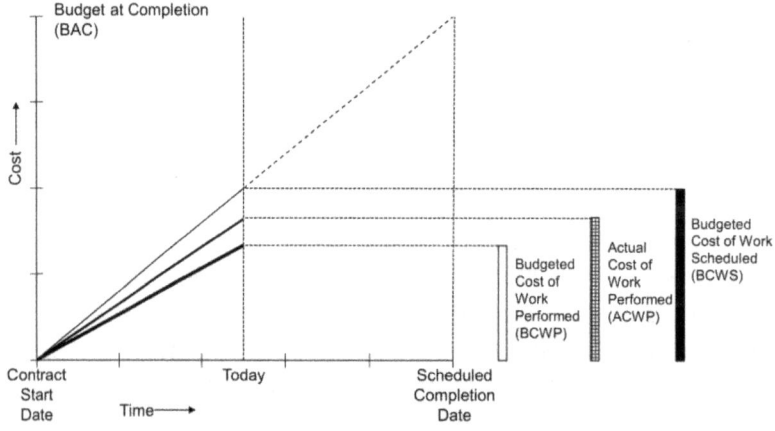

Figure 28. Example of BCWS, ACWP, and BCWP all Growing at Different Linear Rates.

To see things more clearly let's define some terms. We have three basic concepts:

Planned Value (PV)

> The work that was expected to be accomplished for a given amount of money.

Earned Value (EV)

> The work that was actually accomplished, which we just defined as the Budgeted Cost of Work Performed (BCWP).

Actual Cost (AC)

> The money that was actually spent doing the work, which we just defined as the Actual Cost of Work Performed (ACWP).

We will also define the difference between the planned value and actual value as the variance. We have two variances:

Cost Variance (CV)

> $= EV - AC \quad = BCWP - ACWP$

Schedule Variance (SV)

> $= EV - PV \quad = BCWP - BCWS$

Note that SV is measured in cost, not days. It is a measure of how much cost it will take to get back on schedule.

Finally, we define two performance indices that measure the relative deviation between the actuals and the plan:

Cost Performance Index (CPI)

> $= EV / AC \quad = BCWP / ACWP$

Schedule Performance Index (SPI)

> $= EV / PV \quad = BCWP / BCWS$

As can easily be seen, if the performance index is equal to 1.0, then the program is earning value exactly as predicted. If the performance index is less than 1.0, then the program is earning value less efficiently than planned. If the performance index is greater than 1.0, then the program is earning value more efficiently than planned. The cost and schedule variance is illustrated in Figure 29. Plugging in actual numeric values would allow us to calculate CPI and SPI. Based on the relative size of the BCWS, ACWP, and BCWP columns, in this example CPI = 0.80 and SPI = 0.66.

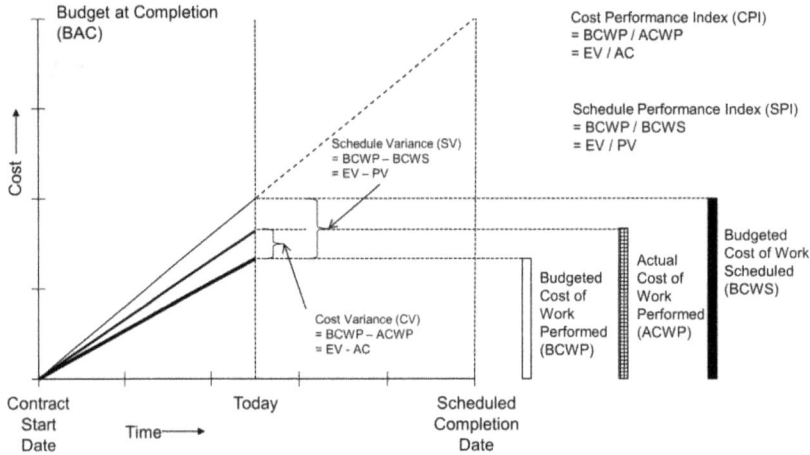

Figure 29. Cost and Schedule Variance.

As is easy to understand, if nothing improves the program will come in over budget and behind schedule as shown in Figure 30. The project continues until the work performed equals 100% of the work planned. At that point in time the ACWP will have exceeded the BAC. The cost overrun is known as the Variance at Completion (VAC). The original BAC plus the VAC sum to the Estimate at Completion (EAC). The Estimate to Completion (ETC), the amount of money needed to finish the project, is also shown.

The difference in time between the scheduled completion date and the projected completion date is the schedule overrun – now measured in actual time – is shown at bottom right. At this point the SV is zero because 100% of the project is complete – all of the value has been earned.

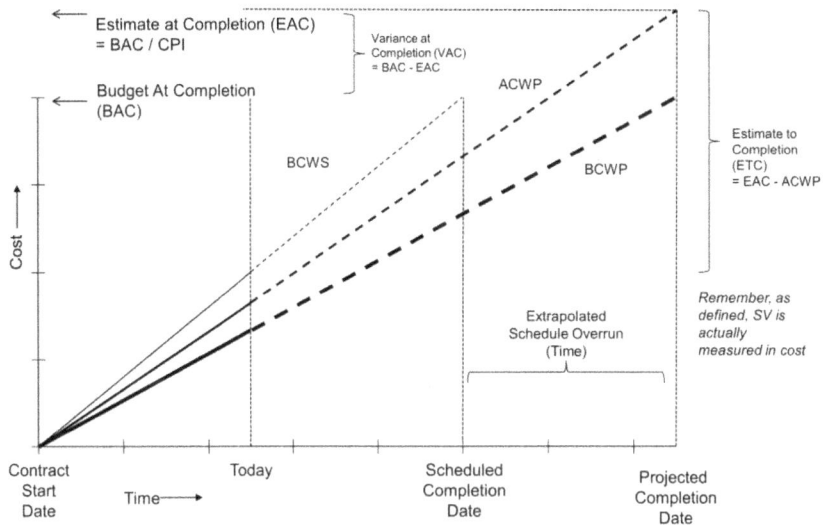

Figure 30. Cost and Schedule Overruns.

Performance indicators are quite useful, but CPI and SPI are indicators of how your program has performed up to that point in time. They tell you if you are behind schedule or over budget. If that happens, you will want to come up with a plan to get back on track. But first, we need to appreciate just how difficult it may be to get things back on track.

We also define the "To Complete" performance indices – a measure of the performance required to complete the program per the original plan. These are:

To Complete Cost Performance Index (TCPI)

= (BAC – EV) / (BAC – AC)

= (BAC – BCWP) / (BAC – ACWP)

To Complete Schedule Performance Index (TSPI)

= (BAC – EV) / (BAC – PV)

= (BAC – BCWP) / (BAC – BCWS)

In order to bring the program in on time and on budget, a significant improvement in performance is required as shown in Figure 31. Based on the relative size of the columns we can see that TCPI = 1.15 and TSPI = 1.34.

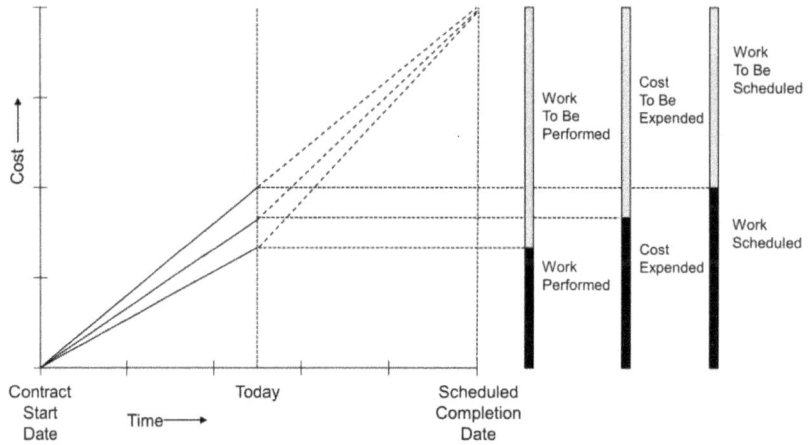

Figure 31. Work to be Performed, Cost to be Expended, and Work to be Scheduled.

Note that the bigger the gap between the Performance Indices and the To Complete Performance Indices, the harder it will be to recover. Time is also a significant factor. A program that is 5% over budget with only 10% of the scheduled time elapsed has 90% of the schedule to adjust it spending and come in on budget. If the same program is 5% over budget with 90% of the schedule elapsed, it will be much more challenging to recover.

MAKING EVM WORK

On a large program, like a new aircraft, the development schedule may take years and cost billions of dollars. Being a million dollars over budget is significant in an absolute sense, but if it represents only 0.1% of the total program budget the resulting CPI at the program level would be

99.9% - a value that most program managers would be very happy with. But we're still a million dollars over budget. How would we know where the problem is? To figure this out cost and schedule must be tracked at a very low level. Low enough that you can see the performance on the individual tasks staffed by a handful of people. The total amount of work is decomposed into small work packages that allow the management team to track overall program performance effectively. This decomposition is shown in Figure 32.

Total Program Cost (TPC)

This is the ultimate cost to the individuals paying for the work. For a commercial program, it may be the company shareholders. On a Government program, this is the tax payers. We have colored these first two boxes in gray to make it clear that there may be a difference between the total cost of the system, and the amount of the contract awarded to the developer. That difference is the contingency / or direct costs.

Contingency / Direct Costs

This is the funding held back by the awarding agency, (e.g., the Department of Defense), to pay their personnel, manage risk or deal with other contingencies. A contractor may win a billion-dollar contract for a major system acquisition, but the government personnel managing the procurement also have to get paid and that adds to the total program cost.

Contract Price

The amount of funding that is awarded to a contractor for a specific amount of work.

Profit / Fee

The amount of profit or fee charged. As we saw in Chapter 2, the fee is typically a percentage of the overall program cost, and the contractual vehicle. We note that the company does not plan to spend this fee as part of the contract execution, so it is not part of the baseline.

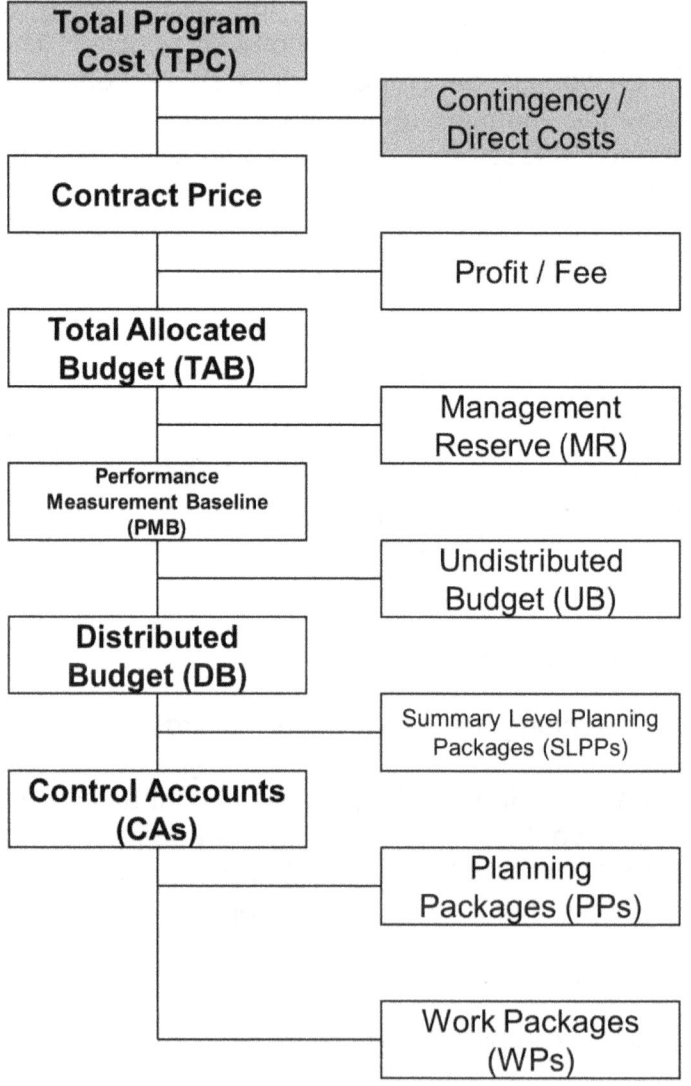

Figure 32. Decomposition of Total Program Cost into Work Packages.

Total Allocated Budget (TAB)

The amount of funding that the project can spend without going over budget. This is the budget project management uses as the starting point for leadership decisions. This is the amount that the program can spend without going over budget.

Since its part of the baseline, you plan to spend it right? Wrong. Stuff happens. Something will go wrong on almost any program. We just don't know what will go wrong or when. To deal with stuff when it happens we withhold management reserve.

Management Reserve (MR)

A low level of funding held back to manage risk, accommodate increases in hourly rates, etc.

Most programs hold back some MR to deal with stuff that will go wrong. If they didn't have a way of dealing with it at the program level, they'd have to go back to the corporation and ask for more money everything something went wrong. MR allows the program to deal with most issues at the program level without impacting other programs.

How much MR should we hold back? There's no consensus, but the answer clearly depends on the level of "risk" associated with the program. The more the risk, the greater the MR withholding. We know of no rigorous studies used to justify the value that is best, but 10% seems to be a reasonable starting point.

Performance Management Baseline (PMB)

The amount of funding that a program plans to spend in executing the work. All future progress will be measured relative to the baseline plan.

Depending on the nature of the program, the entire PMB

may be directly split into individual work packages. Usually this would happen on smaller value, shorter duration, programs. On multi-year, high dollar value programs, not all the PMB may be immediately allocated for work. The PMB can be split into distributed and undistributed budgets.

Undistributed Budget

A temporary holding account for authorized work that has not yet been planned in detail. This funding does not influence resource planning decisions.

Distributed Budget

The amount of funding that has been distributed to specific work elements. This funding does influence resource planning decisions. Again, this may be immediately allocated into individual work packages, but there may also be some intermediate steps.

Summary Level Planning Package (SLPP)

Budget for future work elements, but at a higher level than would be desired for management of active work elements. A temporary holding account for specific in scope work.

Control Account

Work assigned to a specific team, or organization, for a specific amount of work.

Planning Package

A concise work element that has been planned but is far enough in the future that execution does not need to begin in the near term.

This gives the execution team an opportunity to re-examine the plan, before locking the specifics into the financial management system.

Work Package

A concise work element – a specific task or activity – that has been planned and is being executed now or in the very near term. In most companies, work packages are mapped directly to charge numbers that personnel record their time against

Earned value is computed at this level, where the work is actually being performed.

Best Practice Recommendations

To make EVM effective, you should set up the individual work packages at a low enough level to track individual tasks. Have at least one milestone every 2 – 3 weeks and avoid Level of Effort type tasks for most technical work. An exception to that level of effort rule may be for some ongoing work like financial planning, a low level of effort task that must be repeated every month to generate the SPI, CPI values used to determine if the program is on schedule and under budget.

A brief aside here, but defining effective milestones is a bit of an art form on some programs. Some program level milestones may be obvious like – complete the software coding and turn it over to the test group for validation; or attach the wing to the fuselage. But if we're investigating options and our final deliverable is a report that lists the pros and cons of everything we've considered there may not be crisp milestones. In those cases, it may be tempting to create milestones like:

- Turn in Monthly Report for January
- Turn in Monthly Report for February
- Turn in Monthly Report for March

But good milestones should focus on the work itself and not the artifacts of that work. With milestones like "turn in the report" your EVM metrics will always show you as being on schedule as long as you simply turn in the report. But what if the report says, "the building burned down and we have to start over"? That reality should translate into an SPI that tells you the work is behind schedule, but if the value was assigned to turning in the report, it won't. Similarly, if the report says "we had a major breakthrough and trimmed a million dollars off the budget" you won't get any credit for it, because again the value was tied to delivering a report, an artifact, and not completing actual work.

Taking a step back and looking at EVM in general, we can appreciate that it is a useful tool that can – when implemented correctly – give the execution team great insight as to how the team is performing with regard to cost and schedule in relation to the work being performed. The downside is that it is often a non-trivial task to set up intelligent work packages that allow you to measure EVM accurately. It is not always possible to define accurate milestones for work that won't start for several months. (One reason that some work is held in planning packages, instead of immediately defined as work packages.) It's easy to think that work that is highly iterative in nature – like Agile software development tasks – don't easily map into an EVM methodology. But my company uses an Agile software development process, and EVM, and it works quite well.

If you're not familiar with Agile software development, the distinction is that with a traditional waterfall development process, all the features tend to evolve in parallel. Although some parts may evolve at different rates, the program in general would pass through milestones like System Requirements Review (SRR), System Design Review (SDR), Preliminary Design Review (PDR), Critical Design Review (CDR), and so on through Test Readiness Review (TRR) and the final Acceptance Test (AT). With Agile, the features evolve serially.[12] The team agrees on what the

---

[12] For more on Agile see agilemanifesto.org

highest value features are and focuses on taking them all the way through design, development, and acceptance test first, before starting work on lower value features. This is a particularly useful approach for commercial products that have to balance investment and return on investment. You can get high value features ready to deliver early, so you could (in principle) start receiving some revenue, and you add in lower value but nice to have features later. You can still use EVM with an Agile process, because you would only open work packages for the features you're working on now.

PORTFOLIO SUCCESS – BCG MATRIX

If we were to distill down an MBA into one easy lesson it would be – pay attention to your market; your market share; and your margins. One standard way of evaluating all of them at once is a visualization tool developed by the Boston Consulting Group (BCG). The BCG matrix plots the market growth rate on the vertical axis, the market share of a given product on the horizontal axis, uses color coding to indicate the margin of a product, and different size circles to indicate sales.

We'll discuss an example in just a moment, but first a brief aside. Since most of our readers are assumed to have a background in science or engineering, let's ask which way would seem the more obvious way to label the graphs of a 2 x 2 matrix as shown in Figure 33? The only difference is the horizontal axis, which could either run High – Low or Low – High.

Most engineers would naturally default to the option on the right, being accustomed to plotting out numerical values. However, the BCG chose the convention on the left. This makes sense if you intend to label the boxes 1 and 2 on the top, then 3 and 4 on the bottom. Either way works, but if you're like me – when you first see the matrix you catch yourself wondering if they got it backwards. Rather than contribute to the increasing entropy of the Universe, from here on in we will use the approach shown on the right. But please bear in mind that if you find an independent reference to the BCG matrix it will likely follow the convention on the left.

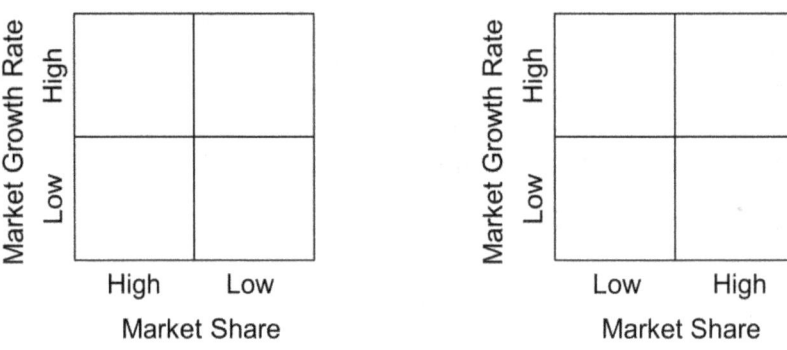

Figure 33. Two Options for Labeling Market Share: High – Low and Low – High.

A notional example of a BCG matrix for eight separate products – products that might make up what is called a portfolio of products – is shown in Figure 34. Let us agree that showing a specific example for a product line from a well-known company would be very helpful. However, it is our experience that company's keep this information very close to home and do not like to make it publicly available. As such, we'll have to make do with a purely notional example.

As shown, there are two products with very high margins, but they are not generating a lot of sales since they are smaller in size. There are two other products with below average margins, and one of them (at upper left) is generating the most in sales since it is the largest size. There is one product with average margins and three other products with above average margins.

Starting with the upper left quadrant, and moving in a clockwise fashion, the four quadrants are notionally referred to as "problem children", "stars", "cash cows" and "dogs" as shown in Figure 35. Let's examine each of these quadrants separately to understand why they have those names.

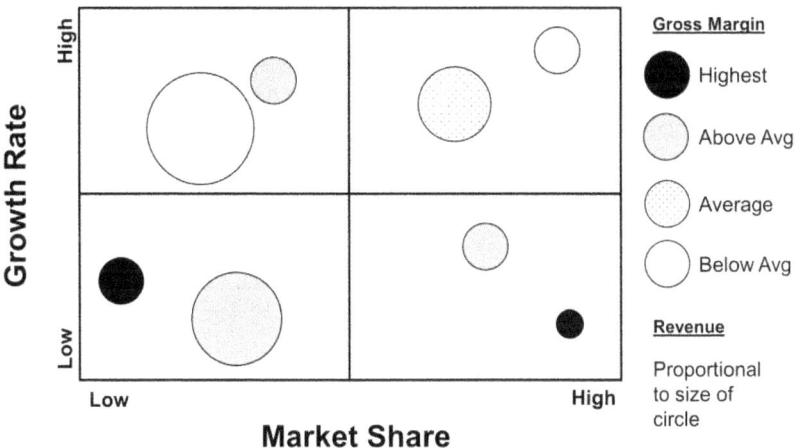

Figure 34. Notional BGC Matrix.

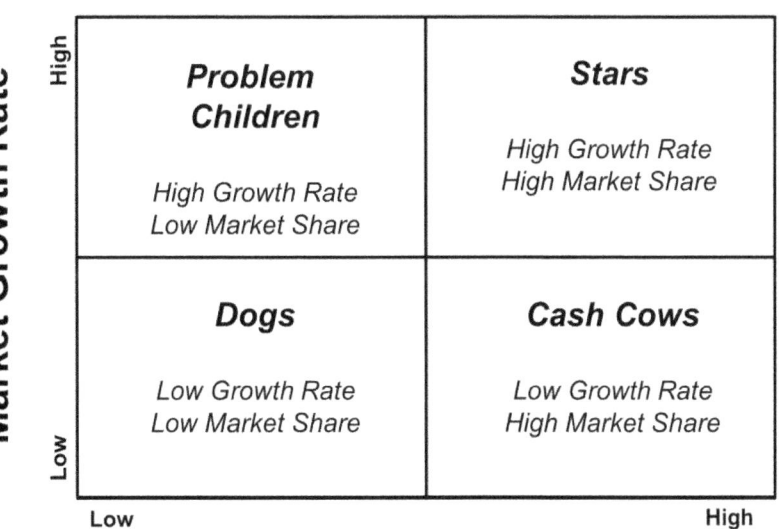

Figure 35. Interpretation of the BCG Matrix.

Problem Children

Problem children are products that are experiencing a high growth rate, which typically requires additional investment in new manufacturing infrastructure to keep up with the demand. But because the market share is low the product line often cannot generate enough cash to keep up. If the market share can be increased, the product can become a star. But if the market growth rate drops, the product will drop to the dogs category. That's what makes this category a problem child, or a question mark. Its not obvious whether they are worth the investment required, but the market growth rate is high enough that its not easy to kill off the product line.

Stars

Obviously, having a high market share in a high growth rate market is a great place to be. Products in that quadrant are called "stars" because they are a shining example of what we wish every product line could be. High market share usually means that products in this category can generate a lot of cash. At the same time, because the market is growing rapidly the company often needs to invest a lot of cash to build the infrastructure necessary to produce the number of products needed. When the market growth rate slows, these products will often drop to the category underneath – that of cash cows.

Cash Cows

Low market growth rate but high market share – these are the cash cows. High market share means high cash flow, and low market growth rate means not much additional investment is required. Cash cows generate more cash than they consume, so the tendency is to continue to "milk" the product line – taking the profit and reinvesting as little as possible. If the business has a few cash cows, they may be able to use that cash to turn problem children into stars. Of course, that same cash could be diverted into dividends for the shareholders, additional research and development, etc.

Dogs

Having a low market share in a low growth rate market is not very attractive. Although the low market growth rate means not much investment is required to keep pace with the competition, the low market share means not much cash is generated. Unless there is reason to believe that the situation will change in the near term, these products are often candidates for divestiture or termination since they seem to have little to offer in the future. Of course, we might make an exception if the product is strategically or tactically important to other parts of the business.

The BCG matrix is a convenient way of examining and evaluating a product family within a given industry, but it is difficult to use for diverse products scattered in different industries. Many large, diversified companies need to do that comparison, hence the need for additional tools.

BUSINESS UNIT SUCCESS – GE / MCKINSEY MATRIX

Another standard example is another matrix developed by McKinsey & Company for General Electric, now known as the GE / McKinsey matrix as shown in Figure 36. This matrix plots business unit strength vs industry attractiveness, often giving each a "high", "medium", or "low" score as opposed to a simple high or low as with the BCG. Each business unit can then be plotted on the graph, once we agree on what we mean by high, medium, or low. Note again that they plotted the horizontal axis backwards from what we scientists and engineers would expect, so we'll change that convention as well going forward.

		Business Unit Strength		
		High	Med	Low
Industry Attractiveness	High	1	2	3
	Med	4	5	6
	Low	7	8	9

Figure 36. GE / McKinsey 3 x 3 Matrix.

Industry attractiveness typically includes market growth rate (the vertical axis for the BCG matrix), but may also include other factors like market size, profitability, competition, global expansion opportunities, and so on. Business unit strength typically includes market share (the horizontal axis for the BCG matrix), but also production capacity, access to distribution channels, brand equity, and so on.

Although we could apply the same terminology used in the BCG matrix evaluation – stars, problem children, dogs, or cash cows – often the decision of what to do with a business unit is put into three categories – grow, hold, or harvest, as shown in Figure 37.

Of course, the whole purpose of this evaluation is to determine where to invest in the short term, to improve the odds of long term growth. Toward the upper right are strong businesses in attractive industries that are well positioned for future growth. These businesses are candidate for investment because there's a strong possibility of a good return on that investment. Toward bottom left are weaker businesses in unattractive industries that do not indicate a promising future. These businesses are candidates for divestiture or harvesting of the profits, but rarely for investment. Of course, in the middle are the businesses on the proverbial fence. They may move up and right, or down and left, depending on the market and future investments in the business itself.

	Business Unit Strength		
	Low	Med	High
Industry Attractiveness — High	Hold	Grow	Grow
Industry Attractiveness — Med	Harvest	Hold	Grow
Industry Attractiveness — Low	Harvest	Harvest	Hold

Figure 37. How the GE / McKinsey Matrix is Used.

CORPORATE SUCCESS – STOCK PRICE

Who evaluates companies? The shareholders. They evaluate the company by buying, or selling, shares of stock. Many of the trades are made by individual investors who are – often times – making less than professional decisions. But by number of shares, the most trades are made by institutional investors – professionals who make buy / sell decisions for a living.

In fact, institutional investors that have huge sums of cash to invest are the primary targets for stock transactions. Institutional investors employ full time stock analysts that specialize in researching specific industries and companies. Their "buy / sell" recommendations make or break companies, and the careers of the executives who lead them.

Examples of institutional investors are shown in Table 36. These investors are organizations that trade securities in large enough share quantities or dollar amounts that they qualify for preferential treatment and lower commissions. Institutional investors face fewer protective regulations because it is assumed that they are more knowledgeable and better able to protect themselves.

Individual stock prices can be influenced by a wide variety of things, but in general shareholders are interested in two key factors

- Financial performance of the company
- Market conditions

As we saw in the sections on Stock Markets and Financial Accounting, the key financial performance metrics are tied to concepts like orders, sales, profit, assets, debt, and so on. Those metrics are an indication of how well the company has done in the recent past and is expected to do in the near future. The market conditions come into play when shareholders ask if that trend is expected to continue, improve, or degrade, in the future. If market conditions are good, or expected to improve, investors tend to feel more confident. If market conditions are poor, or expected to degrade, investors tend to feel less confident.

A good example of the relation between stock prices and the actions of large investors is shown in Figure 38. For the first half of the year, the stock price of the company Weight

Watchers (WTW) was low and slowly varying and on Friday, 16 October 2015 the stock closed at $6.79 per share.

Table 36. Examples of Institutional Investors.

Category	Description
Financial Institutions	This includes commercial banks, investment banks, savings and loans, ... These organizations make loans, pay interest on money deposited, enable wire transfers to other institutions, etc.
Endowment Funds	An endowment is any asset donated to, and for the perpetual benefit of, a non-profit institution. The donation is usually made with the requirement that the principal remain intact and the money earned from investing the principal be used for a specific purpose.
Insurance Companies	Insurance companies mitigate risk by collecting monthly premiums from people / organizations who want to protect themselves against a particular loss (e.g., automobile accident, theft, illness, lawsuit, disability, death, ...). Each month they also pay claims to the, statistically small percentage, of people / organizations that suffer the type of loss they were insured for. The company invests the difference between premium income and claim outgo to ensure long term viability.
Pension Funds	Funds that receive payments from individuals or employers, either public or private; invest the funds; and promise to pay a retirement benefit in the future to the beneficiaries. Pension funds control approximately 40% of all professionally managed assets, worth over $10 trillion.

Figure 38. Weight Watchers (WTW) Stock Price.

Over the weekend an American celebrity, Oprah Winfrey, announced that she was buying a 10% stake in the company. (She also joined the company's board of directors, became a spokesperson for the brand, and went on its diet.)

On Monday morning, 19 October 2015, the stock opened at $11.99 per share. The upward trend continued, and the stock price closed at $18.25 per share on Tuesday, 20 October 2015. People who owned stock on Friday, and held it through Tuesday, saw their investment (potentially) increase by a factor of $18.25 / $6.79 = 269%. The key word is potentially, because to see that increase in your pocket book you would have had to buy at $6.79 and sell at $18.25. Some investors may have been that fortunate, but most bought later, after Oprah made her announcement, or continued to hold onto the stock past the close of business on October 20th. Those who held on were in for a bumpy ride as over the next six months the stock price climbed to a high of $26.61 per share on 18 November 2015 before falling to a new low of $10.03 on 08 February 2016.

Why the big rise? Quite simply because many people believed that Oprah Winfrey had the Midas touch. Products that she endorsed on her television show typically saw big increases in sales. Naturally, it should follow, that if Oprah Winfrey endorses Weight Watchers they should see big increases in their sales, right? Unfortunately, when Weight Watchers reported their fourth quarter 2015 earnings, in early February 2016, they fell short of expectations. Revenue was about 10% lower than projected, and membership had fallen by about 15%. Fail to meet expectations and the stock price often suffers.

Ultimately this is the challenge of managing a successful business. Keep the shareholders happy by showing them a low risk path to short term, and long term, financial growth. Companies that do successfully are rewarded with growing stock prices, and the executives who lead them are referred to by exemplary terms such as "visionary leaders". Companies that don't do this see falling stock prices, and the executives who lead them often have to look for other things to do.

Ask your favorite stock market analyst why any stock, such as Weight Watchers, changes the way it does, and they will probably give you a very detailed, professionally sounding answer. However, we believe a lot of it is simply noise masquerading as signal. We highly recommend the book *Fooled by Randomness: The Hidden Role of Chance in Life and the Markets* by Nassim Nicholas Taleb. The following quote is from the prologue.

> This book is about luck disguised and perceived as non-luck (that is, skills) and, more generally, randomness disguised and perceived as non-randomness (that is, determinism). It manifests itself in the shape of the lucky fool, defined as a person who has benefited from a disproportionate share of luck but attributed his success to some other, generally very precise, reason.
>
> There is one world in which I believe the habit of

mistaking luck for skill is most prevalent – and most conspicuous – and that is the world of markets.

The bottom line – caveat emptor – let the buyer beware.

APPENDIX
LAWS AND REGULATIONS AFFECTING AVIATION AND SPACE EXPLORATION

In this appendix we'll look at how Government laws and regulations impact the aviation and space exploration industries. As we will see, a lot of the terminology that is used within those industries traces back to the Code or CFR.

Wouldn't you agree that if you purchase a ticket on a commercial airline, that you should have a "reasonable" expectation that you would arrive safely at your destination? To ensure the safety of the traveling public, the US government has specified several regulations that companies, or individuals, who wish to provide products and services in this area must abide by. These are summarized in Title 14 of the US Code of Federal Regulations, (see Table 16), which is entitled "Aeronautics and Space.

Civil Aviation and Space

Title 14 is broken into five chapters as shown in Table 37. As shown, this portion of the US CFR specifies the role of the Federal Aviation Administration (FAA), the National Aeronautics and Space Administration (NASA), the Office of the Secretary of the Department of Transportation, and so on. That is, it specifies the authority that the FAA, NASA, etc., have to govern the aeronautics and space industry in the United States.

If you crack open Chapter 1 of Title 14, to look at the Subchapters, you will see that the FAA is authorized to regulate all aspects of US civil aviation. This includes Aircraft, Aircrew, Airlines, Airports, as well as Commercial Space Transportation. So if you want to manufacture aircraft, or supply parts to the aircraft manufacturer, you'd better be familiar with Subchapter C.

Table 37. Title 14 – Aeronautics and Space

Chapter	Description
1	Federal Aviation Administration, Department of Transportation
A	Definitions and Requirements
B	Procedural Rules
C	Aircraft
D	Airmen
E	Airspace
F	Air Traffic and General Operating Rules
G	Air Carriers and Operators for Compensation or Hire: Certification and Operations
H	Schools and Other Certified Agencies
I	Airports
J	Navigational Facilities
K	Administrative Regulations
L	Reserved
M	Reserved
N	War Risk Insurance
2	Office of the Secretary, Department of Transportation
3	Commercial Space Transportation, Federal Aviation Administration, Dept of Transportation
4	National Aeronautics and Space Administration
5	Air Transportation System Stabilization

If you want to be a pilot, you'd better be familiar with Subchapter D. If you want to fly in the National Air Space, you'd better be familiar with Subchapter E, and so on.

Again, just to get a feel for how deep these regulations go, indulge us one other deep dive on Subchapter C. Subchapter C is split into a number of Parts as shown in Table 38. So, if you want to provide parts to an aircraft manufacturer you'd better be familiar with Part 21.

Now this level is deep enough for our purposes, so we'll stop here. But we make the observation that a lot of the terminology we encounter in the commercial aviation industry comes directly from this section of the US CFR. Two terms we hear used liberally in the hallways of aircraft parts manufacturers are Type Certificates and Technical Standard Orders (TSOs). The definitions of those terms are found in the CFR.

> A **type certificate** is issued to signify the airworthiness of an aircraft manufacturing design. The certificate is issued by a regulating body, and once issued, the design cannot be changed.

> A **supplemental type certificate** (STC) is a type certificate (TC) issued when an applicant has received FAA approval to modify an aeronautical product from its original design. The STC, which incorporates by reference the related TC, approves not only the modification but also how that modification affects the original design.

> A **Technical Standard Order (TSO)** is a minimum performance standard for specified materials, parts, and appliances used on civil aircraft.

Table 38. Title 14 Subchapter C – Aircraft.

Part	Description
21	Certification Procedures for Products and Parts
A	General
B	Type Certificates
C	Provisional Type Certificates
D	Changes to Type Certificates
E	Supplemental Type Certificates
F	Production Under Type Certificate
G	Production Certificates
H	Airworthiness Certificates
I	Provisional Airworthiness Certificates
J	Reserved
K	Parts Manufacturer Approval
L	Export Airworthiness Approval
M	Reserved
N	Acceptance of Aircraft Engines, Propellers, and Articles for Import
O	Technical Standard Order Approvals
P	Special Federal Aviation Regulations
23	Airworthiness Standards: Normal, Utility, Acrobatic, and Commuter Category Aircraft
25	Airworthiness Standards: Transport Category Aircraft
26	Continued Airworthiness and Safety Improvements for Transport Category Aircraft

> When authorized to manufacture a material, part, or appliances to a TSO standard, this is referred to as TSO authorization. Receiving a TSO authorization is both design and production approval. Receiving a TSO authorization is not an approval to install and use the article in the aircraft. It means that the article meets the specific TSO and the applicant is authorized to manufacture it.

Similarly, an aircraft manufacturer would also be concerned with obtaining an airworthiness certificate.

> An **Airworthiness Certificate** is an FAA document which grants authorization to operate an aircraft in flight.

The airworthiness standards for further types of aircraft are further defined in Parts 23, 25, 29, and so on.

This level of detail is sufficient to illustrate our original point – the US CFR, or its equivalent in other countries, flows requirements down to manufacturers as a side of effect of the government's role in protecting individual rights. You have the right to expect to arrive safely when you travel to your destination.

Military Aviation

As we just saw, Title 14 contained the regulations on civil aviation in the United States. That seems to raise the question – who regulates military aviation? The answer is – the military services themselves. In the United Kingdom there's a visible Military Aviation Authority (MAA). In the US, each branch of the service does this independently, and the specific source is harder to locate, but the authority is all buried in Title 32 – National Defense.

We won't go into another deep dive on this topic, but we will observe that because the US military is responsible for regulating military aircraft, and that responsibility is separate from the civil regulatory authority, we create the possibility of a disconnect. What happens if the military regulations differ from the civil regulations?

In some cases, the regulations clearly are different – specifically with regard to safety. The good news for the flying public is that the civil regulations are more stringent. That is, civilian aircraft are held to a higher safety standard than are military aircraft. Military aircraft are not designed to transport a civilian population from point A to point B safely; they are designed to support a fighting force that may have to go into harm's way. Still, military aircraft are expected to fly in the same National Air Space as civil aircraft, so in general they follow the same airworthiness standards.

Undoubtedly, there are specific regulations that affect your industry. Make sure you have a high-level understanding of them. In larger companies, there's probably a team of lawyers in the Office of General Counsel (OGC) or certification office that can help.

INDEX

Airworthiness Certificate, 217
Annual Operating Plan, 49 – 52

Business Model, 44 – 47

Capital, 2 – 4
Carnet, 123
Contract Types, 85 – 92
Copyright, 81 – 82
Cost of Money, 38
Cultural Differences, 129 – 133
Currency Exchange Rates, 125 – 128

Direct Commercial Sale, 118
Discretionary Spending, 25 – 28

Economics, definition of, xii
Entrepreneur, 2 – 4
Exchange Rates, see Currency Exchange Rates, 25 – 28
Export Administration Regulations, 119 – 122
Export Regulations, 112 – 122

Federal Acquisition Regulations, 84
Federal Aviation Administration, 55, 97, 213
Fiscal Policy, 107 – 108
Foreign Military Sale, 118 – 119
Future Years Defense Program, 98

Hedge Fund, 127 – 128

Import Regulations, 122 – 125
Intellectual Property, 81 – 84
International Sales Representative, 124, 131
International Traffic in Arms Regulations, 112 – 119

Labor, 1 – 2

Land, 1 – 2
Letter of Agreement, 119
Letter of Request, 119

Market, definition of, 2 – 7
Monetary Policy, 107 – 108

National Aeronautics and Space Administration, 54, 95, 97, 150, 213

Offset, 124

Patent, 67, 81 – 84
Production, Factors of, 1 – 4
Program Element, 100 – 101
Program Objective Memorandum, 99 – 100
Program of Record, 99 – 100

Regulations,
    Export Administration, 112 – 122
    Federal Acquisition, 84
    US Code of, 77 – 80

Small Business, 93 – 94
Stock Market, 10 – 16
Strategic & Financial Plan, 49 – 52

Tax Incentives, 80 – 81
Technical Standard Order, 215
Trademark, 81 – 82
Type Certificate, 215

US Code of Federal Regulations, 77 – 80

Value Proposition, 41 – 44

ACRONYMS

AC	Actual Cost
ACWP	Actual Cost of Work Performed
ARMD	Aeronautics Research Mission Directorate
AUW	Authorized Unpriced Work
B&P	Bid and Proposal
BAC	Budget at Completion
BCWP	Budgeted Cost of Work Performed
BCWS	Budgeted Cost of Work Scheduled
CA	Control Accounts
CBB	Contract Budget Base
CCL	Controlled Commerce List
CEO	Chief Executive Officer
CFO	Chief Finance Officer
CH&MO	Chief Health & Medical Officer
CIO	Chief Information Officer
COO	Chief Operating Officer
CoM	Cost of Money
CoS	Cost of Sales
CPFF	Cost Plus Fixed Fee
CPI	Cost Performance Index
CPO	Chief Procurement Officer
CS&MAO	Chief Safety & Mission Assurance Officer
CS&MO	Chief Strategy & Marketing Officer
CTO	Chief Technology Officer
CV	Cost Variance
DAU	Defense Acquisition University
DB	Distributed Budget
DCS	Direct Commercial Sale
DSP	Department of State Publication
EAC	Estimate at Completion
EAR	Export Administration Regulations
ECCN	Export Control Classification Number

ETC	Estimate to Complete
EV	Earned Value
EVM	Earned Value Management
FAA	Federal Aviation Administration
FABE	Fully Accounted Break Even
FAR	Federal Acquisition Regulations
FFP	Firm Fixed Price
FMS	Foreign Military Sale
G&A	General & Administrative
GDP	Gross Domestic Product
GPR	Government Purpose Rights
HUBZ	Historically Underutilized Business Zone
IDIQ	Indefinite Delivery Indefinite Quantity
IP	Intellectual Property
IR&D	Internal Research and Development
IRR	Internal Rate of Return
ISR	International Sales Representative
ITAR	International Traffic in Arms Regulations
LOA	Letter of Agreement
LOR	Letter of Request
MLA	Manufacturing License Agreement
MR	Management Reserve
NASA	National Aeronautics and Space Administration
NCC	Negotiated Contract Cost
NRE	Non-Recurring Expense
OBS	Organizational Breakdown Structure
OTB	Over Target Baseline
P&L	Profit and Loss
PEL	Permanent Export License
PMB	Performance Management Base

PP	Planning Packages
PV	Planned Value, also Present Value
RE	Recurring Expense
ROI	Return on Investment
SB	Small Business
SDB	Small Disadvantaged Business
SDVOSB	Small Disabled Veteran Owned Small Business
SG&A	Selling, General and Administrative
SLPP	Summary Level Planning Packages
SNLR	Specially Negotiated License Rights
SPI	Schedule Performance Index
SV	Schedule Variance
T&M	Time and Material
TAA	Technical Assistance Agreement
TAB	Total Allocated Budget
TAM	Technical Assistance to Marketing
TAS	Technical Assistance to Sales
TCPI	To Complete Cost Performance Index
TDL	Technical Data License
TEL	Temporary Export License
TPC	Total Program Cost
TSO	Technical Standard Order
TSPI	To Complete Schedule Performance Index
UB	Undistributed Budget
USML	United States Military List
VAC	Variance at Completion
WBS	Work Breakdown Structure
WDA	Warehouse Distribution Agreement
WOSB	Women Owned Small Business
WP	Work Packages

OTHER PUBLICATIONS BY ALAN TRIBBLE

Books

Tribble, A. C., *The Space Environment: Implications for Spacecraft Design*, 2nd Ed., (Princeton, NJ: Princeton University Press, 2003).

Tribble, A. C., *A Tribble's Guide to Space*, (Princeton, NJ: Princeton University Press, 2000).

Tribble, A. C., *Fundamentals of Contamination Control*, (Bellingham, WA: SPIE Press, 2000).

Tribble, A. C., *Princeton Guide to Advanced Physics*, (Princeton, NJ: Princeton University Press, 1996).

Chapters of Books

Tribble, A. C., "Energetic Particles and Technology," in *Heliophysics II - Space Storms and Radiation: Causes and Effects*, Schrijver, C. J., and Siscoe, G. L., (Eds), (Cambridge University Press, 2010).

Tribble, A. C., Hand, K., and Scro, K., "Characterizing Space Weather and its Effects," in *Space Modeling and Simulation*, Rainey, L., (Ed), (Boston, MA: Kluwer Academic Publishers, 2004).

Tribble, A. C., "Effects of the Space Environment," in *Human Space Flight Analysis and Design*, Larson, W., and Pranke, L., (Eds), (Boston, MA: Kluwer Academic Publishers, 1999).

Tribble, A. C., "The Space Environment," in *Spacecraft Mission Analysis and Design*, 3rd Ed., Wertz, J., and Larson, W., (Ed), (Boston, MA: Kluwer Academic Publishers, 1999).

Mendell, W., Plescia, J., and Tribble, A. C., "Surface Environments." in *Human Space Flight Analysis and Design*, Larson, W., and Pranke, L., (Eds), (Boston, MA: Kluwer Academic Publishers, 1999).

www.ingramcontent.com/pod-product-compliance
Lightning Source LLC
Chambersburg PA
CBHW070921030426
42336CB00014BA/2480